Educating the Young Child with Autism Spectrum Disorders

Moving from Diagnosis to Inclusion to Education

by
Michael C. Abraham

illustrated by
Timothy Irwin

Publisher
Key Education Publishing Company, LLC
Minneapolis, Minnesota 55431

www.keyeducationpublishing.com

CONGRATULATIONS ON YOUR PURCHASE OF A KEY EDUCATION PRODUCT!

The editors at Key Education are former teachers who bring experience, enthusiasm, and quality to each and every product. Thousands of teachers have looked to the staff at Key Education for new and innovative resources to make their work more enjoyable and rewarding. Key Education is committed to developing and publishing educational materials that will assist teachers in building a strong and developmentally appropriate curriculum for young children.

PLAN FOR GREAT TEACHING EXPERIENCES WHEN YOU USE EDUCATIONAL MATERIALS FROM KEY EDUCATION PUBLISHING COMPANY, LLC

Credits
Author: Michael C. Abraham
Publisher: Sherrill B. Flora
Project Director: Kelly Gunzenhauser
Creative Director: Annette Hollister-Papp
Illustrations: Timothy Irwin
Cover Design: Annette Hollister-Papp
Editors: Karen Seberg and Claude Chalk
Production: Key Education Production Staff

Key Education welcomes manuscripts and product ideas from teachers. For a copy of our submission guidelines, please send a self-addressed, stamped envelope to:
Key Education Publishing Company, LLC
Acquisitions Department
9601 Newton Avenue South
Minneapolis, Minnesota 55431

About the Author

Michael C. Abraham, has worked closely with children with special needs and served the Fairfield Public Schools for 31 years. He is an honor graduate from Springfield College, and holds advanced degrees from Southern Connecticut State University and Fairfield University. As a nationally recognized Certified Adapted Physical Educator, his mission has always been a "kids come first" approach in their education. Mike has presented numerous professional development workshops to assist and support teachers as they attempt to educate children with special needs within the general education program. Whether working in the aquatic program teaching therapeutic techniques to assist physically challenged children, or working closely with general education classroom teachers demonstrating how children with fine motor and sensory integration difficulties can access the curriculum, Mike has brought his expertise in all endeavours with the child's best interest first. In addition to his "regular" responsibilities, Mike has also served as the district instructor, assisting teachers with developing strategies and techniques to manage student's behaviors when they escalate to include an aggressive verbal and/or physical component. Mike has published numerous books and articles in the areas of special education, adapted physical education, movement and music, and sensory integration.

Dedication

To my very special friend of 25 years, Anthony—all your experiences, both positive and negative, and, most importantly, your thirst for survival in the world of autism have been my teacher. May God bless you.
 —Michael C. Abraham

Special Thanks to Cindy Hoffkins, a Speech and Language Pathologist for Fairfield, CT Public Schools.

Standard Book Number: 978-1-602680-20-3
Educating the Young Child with Autism Spectrum Disorders
Copyright © 2008 by Key Education Publishing Company, LLC
Minneapolis, Minnesota 55431

Printed in the USA • All rights reserved

Contents

Introduction

If you are a teacher, chances are you will have some exposure to students with autism spectrum disorder (ASD). The words *spectrum disorder* mean that every child's symptoms are different and that each child is affected to a varying degree. ASD affects how children (and adults) relate to the outside world—in other words, every aspect of daily life. Most children with ASD have auditory/verbal, visual/spatial, and motor processing difficulties that make everyday interactions challenging, even when they are communicating with very competent teachers (and often, parents).

This book is designed to help you understand and educate children with ASD. There is no magic formula for helping them learn to communicate or for moving beyond this into the curriculum. Most children with ASD can accomplish skills at their own pace and with different rates of success. Finding out what each child needs, using appropriate intervention strategies, and maintaining patience are the keys to reaching each of them. A child with ASD must rely on competent, caring teachers to establish a two-way relationship by following the child's lead; by supporting his spontaneity and internal motivation; by assisting the child to communicate; and, by helping him encounter and understand a range of feelings. All of these goals can be accomplished while he is interacting with peers and working on curriculum-based skills. An effective teacher becomes part of the child's world, understands his distinctiveness, and finds ways to comfort him.

Chapter One
About Autism Spectrum Disorders

For educators facing the likelihood of integrating children with Autism Spectrum Diso[r]
into their classrooms, some general information is helpful. Autism was first described in 1[?]
by psychiatrist Leo Kanner and again in 1944 by Austrian pediatrician Hans Asperger. Au[t]
Spectrum Disorders (ASD) are actually a range of disorders—Autism, Asperger's Disorder, Childh[o]
Disintegrative Disorder, Pervasive Developmental Disorder Not Otherwise Specified (PDDNOS),
and Rett's Disorder that vary in severity, symptoms, and age of onset. Some indications are that one
in 166 people has ASD. It is 3 to 4 times more likely to affect boys and 50 times more frequent in
siblings of those already affected.

ASD is believed to stem from a chain of events that may involve a combination of abnormal
genes and chromosomes, metabolic disorders, viral agents, immune intolerance, and anoxia (oxygen
deprivation). These factors cause changes in brain development, which result in atypical cognitive
and social development. ASD affects individuals uniquely. Most will exhibit the characteristics to
varying degrees throughout their lifetimes. There is currently no cure, but various therapies have led
to positive changes in the lives of people with ASD.

Diagnosing a Child with ASD

The Diagnostic and Statistical Manual of Mental Disorders (DSM-TR), published by the American
Psychiatric Association, names five deficit areas to consider as diagnostic criteria: **communication**,
socialization and social skills, **restricted interests**, **sensory integration**, and **behavior**.

Research has also indicated four early indicators for diagnosing ASD:

1. **lack of eye contact,**

2. **lack of joint attention** (the process of engaging in shared attention to an object or event by
   following and initiating pointing or gaze gestures, and of being aware of, and enjoying, that
   shared attention),

3. **lack of reciprocal conversation** (no babbling by 12 months or words by 16 months or loss
   of speech or social skills at any time), and

4. **atypical sensory/motor processing** (a deficiency in how the brain interprets and prioritizes
   information gathered by the senses).

In addition to these early indicators, which often remain present, other characteristics may
include:

- Impaired ability to form social and emotional relationships

- Repetitive, non-goal-directed body motions and behaviors (such as rocking)

- Resistance to, or distress at, changes in environment or routines

- Abnormal perceptual and motor experiences (such as "looking through" people)

- Not seeing certain objects

- Not hearing some sounds and overreacting to other areas

- Walking on tiptoes

- Hyperactivity or passivity

- Severe speech impairment and language difficulties

- Retardation in some areas, often accompanied by superior skills in others

- Excessive preoccupation with certain objects

- Lack of awareness of body and body part functions

- Difficulty with identifying important global concepts and elements of tasks

- Difficulty processing auditory information: poor ability to understand, retain, and retrieve information (For example, a child can repeat information but cannot apply it.)

- Difficulty with generalizing skills; skills must be taught in context (For example, a child can tie his shoes with coaching from an occupational therapist but not with others or on his own.)

- Difficulty with sequencing information or steps

- Difficulty with time concepts and time management

- Atypical or uneven academic, social, or emotional development

- Difficulty regulating emotions

- Difficulty reading or imitating facial expressions and body language

- Limited awareness of how a conversation is supposed to work (wait time and giving and getting information)

- Difficulty with learning by listening

- Biting, scratching, or self-injury when faced with a stressful situation

- Generally slow progress

This list shows that attending school has several purposes for the child with ASD, including overcoming some of the sensory/motor roadblocks to communication, replacing certain behaviors with others, learning to build relationships with teachers and peers, and learning curriculum-area subject matter. Finding the best environment for the child with ASD to accomplish these broad goals is the job of the people who form the individualized education program (IEP) team. (See page 8 for more about the IEP process.)

Chapter Two
Assessment and the Individualized Education Program (IEP): An Overview

The Individuals with Disabilities Education Act (IDEA) is a federal law that requires the public education system to provide appropriate educational services to children with disabilities. IDEA lists the following three steps that begin the process of educating each child with a disability:

1. Professionals within the school system identify children who are eligible for special education services.

2. A team assesses each child's abilities and develops an individualized education program (IEP) that states goals for the child's education.

3. The IEP team determines the least restrictive environment (LRE) in which the goals and objectives on the IEP can be attained.

Step 1: Identifying Children with ASD

While this book deals primarily with what happens after a child with ASD is referred for special services, it is helpful to understand the whole process. IDEA requires school systems to identify infants and toddlers who display developmental delays and qualify for early intervention. IDEA also requires evaluation of children ages 3–21 for eligibility for special services. Many people can refer children for evaluations, including parents, doctors, hospitals, child care workers, public schools, public health facilities, social service agencies, and any other agency that receives public funds.

Certain principles should govern the assessment of a child who has been referred.

- **First, multiple areas must be assessed (intellectual and communicative skills, behavioral presentation, and functioning skills).**

- **Second, the child's behavior on assessment will vary depending on novelty, structure, and complexity of the environment.**

- **Third, skills demonstrated in more highly structured situations must be viewed in the broader context of a child's typical performance.**

- **Fourth, social dysfunction is a defining feature of ASD and must be considered.**

- **Fifth, behavioral difficulties must be examined since they affect the child's academic and social functioning.**

(Step 2: The IEP Process — Forming the IEP Team, found on the following page, may be duplicated and given to parents as an informational resource.)

Step 2: The IEP Process—Forming the IEP Team

Once the school system identifies a child in need of special services, an IEP team is formed. It should include most of the following people.

Who's Who on IEP Teams

- **Parents** should attend all IEP meetings. They may not (yet) be experts on ASD, but they are experts on their child. The child should attend if appropriate.

- **School psychologists** usually perform the child's initial evaluations (IQ, achievement, autism assessments, rating scales, social developmental history, etc.). They may assist with classroom interventions and help parents find appropriate outside resources for treatment, medical intervention, counseling, support groups, and confirmation of the diagnosis.

- **Special education teachers** primarily teach classrooms of children with disabilities, can teach life skills and social skills, and can help the general education teacher adapt the curriculum. A child with ASD may divide his time between a special classroom and a regular classroom.

- **Case managers lead IEP teams.** (The special education teacher may also be the case manager, but not always.) They monitor whether supplementary aids and services are helping to educate the child, and they also use predetermined criteria to measure each child's progress toward the IEP goals and objectives.

- **Paraprofessionals** form a bridge between children with ASD and teachers, students, and administrators. They may modify curriculum materials, help classmates relate to the child, and meet with the teacher to set goals and evaluate progress. They often "shadow" children who need help with behavior control. Shadows may be screened and hired by parents rather than the school system.

- **Educational trainers** can administer the applied behavior analysis (ABA) program altering the child's environment until a desired behavioral change occurs and collects data to document results. They can train other staff to apply the ABA program as well as modify curriculum based on IEP goals and perform duties of the special education teacher when she is not available.

- **Physical therapists** help children with ASD achieve normal motor skills. PTs may create sensory diets (a physical activity regimen; see pages 37–43) for children who need help in regulating sensory input.

- **Occupational therapists** help children with ASD learn life skills like communication, dressing, transitioning between situations, and job skills.

- **Professional advocates** and **legal representatives** are often hired by parents to attend meetings and act on their behalf. Advocates should meet the IDEA criteria for team member eligibility: "knowledgeable about the child, the meaning of the evaluation data, and the placement options" (Sec. 300.552 Placements).

How IDEA Governs IEP Teams

IDEA affirms that "to the maximum extent appropriate, children with disabilities, including children in public or private institutions or other care facilities, are educated with children who are nondisabled" and also that "special classes, separate schooling or other removal of children with disabilities from the regular educational environment occurs only if the nature or severity of the disability is such that education in regular classes with the use of supplementary aids and services cannot be achieved satisfactorily." (Authority: 20 U.S.C. 1412 (a)(5)) The key words here are "maximum extent appropriate." Each IEP team is formed to find out to what extent a child can be educated with nondisabled peers and what must happen to make that possible.

Initial Assessment of the Child

This IEP team assesses the child's needs and then designs an education program that is unique to that child. The *I* in IEP stands for individualized. It is the child who is being assessed, not the disability label. All children on the autism spectrum function and perform differently. The team must consider the child's strengths and weaknesses, how the particular disability affects the child's communication and learning, and also what the parents want for their child and what the child wants for herself. The IEP team must then determine the following:

- Current performance levels
- Benchmarks and goals and how progress toward them will be measured
- What services are to be provided, on what schedule, and for what duration
- What classroom and curriculum modifications are needed
- When and why a child will be removed from his peers, if at all
- Whether it is possible to set goals for middle school, high school, and beyond

The Least Restrictive Environment (LRE)

The LRE is the most "normal" setting in which the child can achieve the IEP goals. An environment in which the child participates fully with nondisabled peers is considered unrestricted. Special education classes, special schools, and institutional environments are considered more restrictive, as is any time that a child is kept from participating in the regular classroom. Placement is based on the child's profile (academic, behavioral, and social/emotional considerations; and other information like his impact on the LRE and how his disability affects his progress), as well as the feasibility of modifications and accommodations that must be made to the LRE and curriculum in order to include the child. A *modification* is any change made to the regular curriculum due to the child's disability, such as a change in the number of skills taught or use of a parallel curriculum. An *accommodation* is a change to the environment, materials, or assignments that does not change the curriculum content. Accommodations establish a level playing field by insuring that the child's performance reflects knowledge, understanding, or application of the material rather than the impact of the disability on the assignment. Examples include offering materials on audiotape or changing the appearance (not the content) of a worksheet. If accommodations and modifications are too extreme to allow the classroom to function normally, or if the curriculum must be altered so greatly that it is unrecognizable, then a more restrictive environment is appropriate.

The intent of IDEA is to educate disabled children with nondisabled peers as much as possible. IDEA assumes that the IEP team looks at the general education classroom as its first LRE option. But, if the team determines that a child cannot be educated satisfactorily in a regular classroom, even with supplementary services, that child can be placed in another setting for instruction, such as a special education class or school, the home, or a hospital or institution. More restrictive environments may indeed be appropriate; the goal is to find the most "normal" setting that works for the child with ASD.

Step 3: Aligning the Potential LRE to the Child's Assessment

Once the child with ASD has been assessed, the team must then make specific recommendations for the least restrictive environment. Fortunately, there is room to be flexible and creative in making modifications and accommodations to the regular education classroom in order to meet the child's needs. Teams should look at overall school environments as well as classrooms and teachers. They should strive to agree on the definition of appropriateness as they consider all of the following factors.

LRE Considerations: Child

- What is the present level of performance for the whole child (physical and emotional make-up and readiness to learn academic material)?

- Will the amount of assistance that the child requires be appropriate for the proposed LRE?

- Does the child possess the endurance and muscle strength to participate fully in the potential LRE?

- Will the LRE have a positive impact on the child's self-esteem and self-image?

- Is there a difference between the child's chronological vs. developmental age? Does the child possess age-appropriate social behaviors and skills? How do these factors impact the LRE decision?

- Does the child take medication with side effects that may interfere with his participation in the proposed LRE?

- What other personal factors (diet, sleeping patterns, general health, expressive language skills, emotional stability and family dynamics) may impact the child's performance in the LRE?

LRE Considerations: Parents

- What do the parents want for their child? (IEP teams should take parents' input into consideration, but the process should not be driven by them.)

- Can the parents reinforce at home the learning that will take place in the LRE?

- Does the child need more of a functional education that teaches life skills? (Parents need to address this issue regularly. This component may be controversial, for it asks the school system to be a partner in teaching more than just the curriculum. If IEP teams agree to adapt this mind-set, the IEP can focus on improving the child's life skills as well as his education.)

LRE Considerations: Staff and Services

- Are the general education teachers in the LRE a good fit for the child in terms of their teaching styles, professional training, and knowledge of ASD?

- Will the general education teacher attend IEP meetings to offer insight into the classroom environment, pace of instruction, and subject matter?

- Are the general education teacher and other staff trained to implement special education strategies for the child with ASD? Is ongoing training in place?

- Are there knowledgeable special education administrators at the school who can moderate the IEP meeting and support its decisions?

- Where are the special educators located in the building? Is the staff sufficient to meet the needs of all enrolled children with disabilities?

- What additional staff members (paraprofessionals, occupational therapists, physical therapists, etc.) are available? What are their roles?

LRE Considerations: Budget

- Even though IDEA states that each disabled child who qualifies is entitled to a free appropriate education, can the IEP team still make an appropriate plan considering the LRE and budget implications? The difference between what the school system and IEP team deem "appropriate" and the "maximum benefit" sought by parents often causes tension. Parents want what will bring about the most positive change for their child, and under the wording of IDEA, they feel entitled to it. However, school systems can successfully argue that the child is in an appropriate environment, even if every benefit parents seek is not provided. Part of the IEP team's job is to find creative ways of providing what is best for the child, even in the face of tight budgets and limited resources.

LRE Considerations: LRE Environment

- Is the classroom a stable environment? Is the environment too stimulating or not stimulating enough for the child with ASD? Can it be made more appropriate?

- Does the overall campus provide the proper setting for the child?

- Will the child be educated with nondisabled peers to the maximum extent appropriate?

LRE Considerations: LRE Curriculum

- Is the curriculum's pace, language, and subject matter developmentally appropriate for the child? If not, can it be modified or can a meaningful parallel curriculum be created to meet the child's needs and the goals of the IEP team?

- Does the curriculum suit the child's learning style and cognitive abilities?

Goals and Future Considerations

What is the definition of success? Is it socialization? Academic growth? How will goals be measured? Choosing immeasurable goals is a pitfall for IEP teams because some team members may feel an objective has been met, while others do not, and there is often no hard data to determine who is correct. Therefore, goals and specific ways to measure progress need to be stated. For example, in addition to listing the goal of "Jeffrey will show understanding of cause-and-effect relationships," the IEP should give specific examples of how the team will know when this goal has been met:

- **Ask for specific snack foods by name before being rewarded (75% accuracy).**

- **Turn on his special reading light without prompting when the classroom is darkened (50% accuracy).**

- **Raise his hand when he has a question (50% accuracy).**

In addition, IEP teams must look at the measurable goals over time. Deciding exactly what will be measured is a lot of work up front, but it is far easier to do this than to look back on Jeffrey's performance and debate whether or not he understands cause and effect. As long as someone records notes about how many times Jeffrey asks for foods by name, turns on his light, and raises his hand, his progress will be a documented fact.

- **Can goals realistically be met in one school year?**

- **Are goals indeed being met? (If the child is not progressing toward the goals on the IEP, then they need to be revisited. If the goals are still appropriate, the current LRE is probably not the best environment for the child.)**

- **Has the team considered the impact of the present LRE on next year's placement?**

These are broad categories. When IEP teams convene they must consider specific strategies (covered in subsequent chapters) that will take place each day to help the child with ASD to be successful in the LRE. These include modifying classrooms and curriculum, adjusting teaching styles, creating sensory diets and behavior modification plans, and fostering socialization. Because the best IEPs are very specific, team members are encouraged to read ahead in order to make decisions about what modifications and accommodations are possible in order to include the child with ASD in the regular classroom.

A Special Word about Working with Parents

Working with parents of a child with ASD can be inspiring or exhausting. Even the most helpful parents are often consumed with managing their child's issues and trying to learn the new role of advocacy. Parenting a child with ASD can be overwhelming and is often so challenging it can effect the overall family dynamic. There is a great push to educate these children in the curriculum; however, parents also have to ask questions such as, "How will he function in society? Can he learn how to care for himself? Can he find a job or live independently? Will he have friends? Will our lives ever return to normal?"

Parents may be very involved, dominant, and knowledgeable about their child and continually communicate with the school to "make sure" the program is right. Other parents may be supportive and reliable, ask good questions, and support the program at home. Still other parents are very passive and seem uninvolved or incapable of dealing with their child's problems. But, more than anyone else, parents can make a world of difference in helping the child with learning or behavior problems. Other IEP team members should make every effort to encourage parents to be a productive part of the team.

Tips for Working Closely with Parents to Develop the Best Educational Plan

- Communicate frequently and openly with parents. Encourage them to express their wants as you express your observations so that both parties are fairly represented. Parents should not dictate, and teachers should not resist new ideas.

- Invite parents into the classroom. They will receive a vast amount of information as they watch their child learn. It will also assist them when they need to discuss which setting would be best to attain the goals and objectives on the IEP. Placement is often controversial, emotional, and difficult to understand in the abstract, especially if the LRE is not found to be a regular classroom. Seeing their child in different environments will help parents make the best choices.

- Be direct and professional when providing information. "Tell it like it is" since what you do or do not say at a meeting can affect a child's education for months or longer.

- Demonstrate to parents that you care about and want to do the best for their child.

- Collect information from parents about the family's dynamics so that you can better understand how the child functions at home and how those issues may impact his performance at school.

- Finally, help parents "get their feet wet" by referring them to Appendix A: The IEP Meeting— Helpful Hints for Parents of Children Who May Be on the Autism Spectrum.

A Final Word about IEP Meetings

The IEP team needs to make finding the most appropriate education plan for the child their one goal. Due to emotional issues and budgetary concerns, sometimes teams do not proceed with this one goal in mind, and the child may then inherit a program that is not in his best interests. If team members separate in their beliefs, parents and schools have due process rights at that time to resolve their differences.

To avoid getting to this point, the IEP team should not begin with the assumption that the appropriate LRE is the regular classroom. Instead, the team should visualize the child as a pendulum. Far to the left is the general education classroom and far to the right is the special education classroom. The pendulum—the child—starts at the center. When the IEP team begins discussing the child's program, this pendulum will begin to "swing" from side to side. A team member may suggest that the child can achieve some goals in the regular education classroom, and the pendulum will swing to the left. Then, another member may present other goals, and the team may decide that these cannot be achieved in the regular education classroom, even with supplementary services, and should occur in a more restricted environment. At that time the pendulum will swing back to the right. This process will take place many times throughout the meeting. If IEP members keep open minds and focus on the child, the pendulum will come to rest at the best place for the child by the end of the meeting.

Chapter Three
Moving beyond the IEP Meeting into the Classroom

Many decisions about educating the child with ASD can be made in initial IEP meetings. Thorough preparation in these meetings will help your school year start smoothly. You have probably started educating yourself by reading current literature and attending workshops given by experts on ASD. You have probably familiarized yourself with the characteristics and behaviors of your specific student through IEP meetings and reviewing previous IEPs. Hopefully, you have asked the child's parents questions like, "What type of home environment does the child come from? What experiences has he had? What type of sensory stimuli impacts his performance? What motivates him?" The more information you have, the better the program the IEP team will design for the child, and the easier time you will have teaching the child and troubleshooting problems.

The remaining chapters in this book have two purposes. First, refer to these chapters before the initial IEP meeting as a reminder of the vast range of considerations for things that can appear on the IEP. Second, use the chapters to help you troubleshoot problems that crop up during the school year. One of the great things about the IEP process is that a child's plan can be revisited and adjusted at any time. Obviously, it is best to prepare yourself and the classroom ahead of time as much as possible; not only will you feel more prepared, but the children in your classroom will be unaware that things are different because of the child with ASD. However, you do not have to do everything at once, and you will not know everything you need to know for the IEP until you see how the child reacts to the LRE.

As the child with ASD progresses in the LRE, the primary focus remains to monitor the measurable goals and objectives and how they are being achieved. The planned accommodations and modifications within the LRE that are specifically addressed in subsequent chapters must address IEP goals and objectives. These goals may include, but are not limited to, making the classroom and the curriculum accessible, ensuring ongoing acquisition of functional communication, and consistently monitoring and assessing behaviors that may interfere with the LRE environment and the child's learning. As you read ahead to find out how to implement and adjust many of the possible recommendations from a child's IEP, here are some basic principles to follow:

1. **Treat all children with dignity and respect.**

2. **Establish rapport, build trust, and attempt to maintain eye contact with the child when possible.**

3. **Use repetition, continuity, and experience as foundations for future learning.**

4. **Build on the child's strengths, rather than focusing on weaknesses.**

5. **Remind yourself that there is never a right or wrong expectation. Rather, the outcome should be a positive experiential encounter within the LRE.**

6. **Always provide immediate positive reinforcement for a desired behavior.**

7. **Changes implemented should be student oriented, not curriculum based. Make the program fit the child as much as possible.**

8. **Remember, all of the children you teach are just young kids. Have FUN!**

Chapter Four
The Learning Environment:
Adjusting the Classroom and the Curriculum

Once you know the child, the IEP goals, and the available resources, you can plan a classroom that acts as a "home base"—a safe, predictable place from which the child with ASD can integrate into the larger school environment. It is not practical or desirable to implement every idea in this chapter; however, great effort should be made to create a workable environment for the child.

The Classroom

First, look at your classroom. Some environmental aspects can interfere with the child's learning and contribute to undesirable behavior, a topic dealt with extensively in subsequent chapters. Accommodating this child requires rethinking your classroom according to the IEP goals and objectives. Make some changes before the school year begins and other changes as you become familiar with the child.

Noise

Noise can effect concentration for all children. "Normal" sound to you may be too loud or quiet for the child with ASD who has sensory integration issues (difficulty monitoring sensory input). See the chapter titled "Available to Learn: Providing Appropriate Sensory Input" (page 32) for more about sensory integration dysfunction.

- Avoid hallway noise and high-traffic areas (bathroom, water fountain, pencil sharpener) when choosing a seat for the child.

- Let the child use earmuffs or earplugs to block sounds.

- Some children benefit from background noise to filter out intrusive sounds. If the child likes music, place a CD player nearby so it does not bother others or let the child use an MP3 player with white noise or soothing music.

- Try playing classical music to signal the appropriate noise level. When noise drowns out the music, say, "Boys and girls, I cannot hear our music!" to prompt them to lower their voices. They will learn to regulate their own noise levels.

- For some activities, increased volume will enhance learning. Use louder music and perhaps movement: marching, movement games that incorporate academics, or acting out stories and poetry.

- Change the music or the noise level to make transitions more definable and predictable for the child with ASD.

- It may be difficult to maintain quiet. If the classroom gets too loud for the child with ASD, have her leave to take a break.

Smells

Certain odors can cause a child to display inappropriate behaviors. Avoid wearing heavy perfume or using strong air fresheners. Make sure any area where children use paint or markers is well ventilated. Keep the air circulating and the classroom clean.

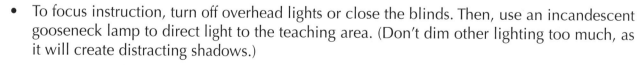

Temperature

Warm temperatures make some children drowsy and others agitated, while cold rooms can make children "huddle" to keep warm. Adjust the temperature as necessary.

- Children often need warmer temperatures than adults.

- Be aware of how changing seasons impact the classroom. A 73°F (23°C) room temperature is not appropriate if it is very cold outside, and children are wearing heavy sweaters.

- Opening a window or turning on a fan may be as effective as air conditioning.

- Teach the life skill of adding and removing layers. Request that parents send in sweaters and dress children in light layers that can be removed.

Lighting

Lighting influences some children's behavior and concentration. You may not have much control over uncomfortable lighting, but here are some hints for what you can do about it:

- How does the light feel to you? Observe the type of lighting throughout the room (natural, fluorescent, lamps) at different times of the day.

- Adapt lighting to the time of the year. In winter months, add more artificial light.

- It is best for natural light to enter from more than one direction. Since the average classroom has windows on only one side, create a balance by adjusting blinds throughout the day. Use translucent curtains and slatted blinds to diffuse light and direct it further into the room, and remove hanging materials from blinds so that you can adjust them as needed.

- Dim lighting makes some children sleepy and sluggish but makes others calm and focused. If the classroom lighting is not appropriate for the child with ASD and cannot be changed, have the IEP team discuss creating a light-friendly area.

- Allow the child with ASD to wear a hat with a brim to diminish desktop glare. Or, get permission to cover overhead lighting with tinted, heat-resistant theatrical lighting gels. For glare on computer screens, move the monitors, top them with commercial glare-reducing screens, or cut apart shoe boxes and tape the long sides over the tops of the monitors.

- Try to reduce harsh shadows near where the child with ASD will sit and where you will be instructing.

- To focus instruction, turn off overhead lights or close the blinds. Then, use an incandescent gooseneck lamp to direct light to the teaching area. (Don't dim other lighting too much, as it will create distracting shadows.)

Other Visual Considerations

Children with ASD can be over- or understimulated by what they can see in a room. Often less is better. Know what the child can tolerate and be aware of the "visual noise" on walls and windows. Use these ideas to tone down or focus visual stimulation.

- Use soft, neutral colors in the classroom to calm children and to enhance attention and focus. Use bright colors sparingly to highlight important areas.

- Store unnecessary or large equipment and materials, like televisions, VCRs, and large pads or rolls of paper, in closed cabinets or outside the classroom.

- Teach in front of a "sterile" background.

- Instead of posting the alphabet, numbers, colors, and shapes on the walls, give each child a laminated notebook containing these items.

- Display children's work in one area that is not near instructional areas. Consider hanging artwork only in the hallway.

- Clear calendars, pictures, word walls, and other distractions from blackboards.

- Present visuals that are necessary for instruction at the child's eye level.

- Use small-scale visual barriers, like a study carrel, when visual noise cannot be removed.

At this point, you may feel that having a child with ASD in your classroom means that you have to have a drab background. Not so. Create a balance for the child with ASD and other children who prefer more visual stimulation by installing clotheslines or long drapery rods. Hang drapes, curtains, or bed sheets in neutral tones. Close them to reduce visual distractions when you are instructing or when you are trying to calm the child with ASD.

Classroom Layout

Children with ASD often have great challenges concentrating and attending to instruction. Thoughtful classroom layout design can help. As you decide what goes where, use these suggestions to enhance children's abilities to attend and focus:

- Leave enough room between desks for children to move without crowding into each other's personal space. If desks must be close together, leave at least a few inches in between and place the desk of the child with ASD at an outside corner.

- Further define personal space by placing masking tape outlines on the floor.

- Dedicate each space in the room to only one use. For example, use one corner just for reading and another only for painting. Limiting the number of activities in each area can help the child with ASD develop transitional and organizational skills.

- Having well-defined spaces may decrease a child's tendency to wander (or run) from area to area. Strategically place furniture to visually define specific areas.

- Further define areas of the room with visual cues. For example, hang a picture of books in the reading area and a picture of blocks in the block area to help each child know what is expected as he moves through the classroom.

- Allow space (or move desks as necessary) so that children can move freely and play movement games. (Some movement games can also incorporate academic themes—a bonus for kinesthetic learners.)

- Keep the physical environment as stable as possible from day to day, especially in the area of the room where the child's desk is located.

- When moving tables or desks, preserve the child's location if possible and prepare the child for her new location if it is truly necessary to move it.

- If it is appropriate, periodically change the location of the child's desk to begin to break the cycle of rigidity. Thoroughly prepare the child for this change.

Desk Placement

For the child with ASD, the location of their desk is very important, especially if she is sensitive to noise or movement or is tactile defensive (highly sensitive to light touch, to the point of fleeing or becoming aggressive).

- If possible, let the child with ASD select her own desk before classmates arrive.

- Place the child's desk in a low-traffic area, away from the wastebasket, pencil sharpener, windows, your desk, and pathways to doors.

- The front row may not be ideal for the child with ASD. He may become the distraction that interrupts the instructional process for everyone else. Consider placing his desk in the back row so that he has access to his sensory break area (see below).

- Make sure the child has a clear line of sight to your instruction areas.

- During large group instruction, stand as close to the child with ASD as possible, even if her desk is in the back row. The physical connection helps the child improve attending skills.

Desk Organization and Materials

What is in and on the child's desk is as important as where the desk is located. Children with ASD can be easily overstimulated by clutter, and they often lack organizational skills. Traditional methods of helping the child with ASD become more organized, such as prompting, can move him to action, but they rarely keep him in motion. Instead of undergoing a lasting change of behavior, the child learns to wait for others to force him into action and has difficulty learning techniques for self-monitoring, self-discipline, initiative, and independence. Therefore, it is important to make sure that organization and maintenance are part of the child's routine from the beginning. The following suggestions can help keep desks and children organized. A paraprofessional can assist the child with these tasks until he can complete them independently.

- If there is space, provide two desks for the child with ASD: one in the large group setting and one in a quiet area. When required to work independently, the child may benefit from working at her other desk in the quiet area.

- Place a small whiteboard on the desk or hang it from a hook. Write the daily schedule, and any changes to it, on the whiteboard. Or, tape a written or picture schedule or calendar to the child's desk. (The schedule should be available to paraprofessionals as they assist the child with classroom routines and transitions.)

- A calendar of assignments and projects, as well as a checklist of the day's activities, should also be taped in the child's notebook or sealed in a clear folder and attached to the desk. Have the child check them off as they are completed.

- Keep supplies in resealable, plastic bags at the child's desk. Provide a flat tray in which to store the bags. (Opening and closing the bags encourages fine motor development and graphomotor skills such as hand strength and tripod grip.) On the desktop, tape a list of materials needed to start each day. Assist the child in gathering these materials until she is able to gather them on her own.

- Use desk dividers to create small cubby areas for materials. Label the dividers or place a picture in the desk to show the child how to store materials.

- Attach magnetic clips to the side of the desk to hold loose papers and work that needs to be completed during the day.

- If a child has a lot of trouble with organization, place a small box or bookshelf next to his desk and store his books, notebooks, and materials in it. In extreme cases, keep the child's materials near your desk. Let him select them as needed.

- Provide duplicate books and supplies for home use to lessen the opportunity for more disorganization. Only send papers home in a closeable folder.

- Remove materials that are unnecessary to the present learning activity or give wait time for the child to transition her own materials.

- Don't let all of this good organization go to waste! Teach the child "how to" place papers in folders and return toys and crayons to their proper places. Ask a paraprofessional to demonstrate cleaning up during a quiet period and reinforce it afterwards by prompting the child as needed.

Alternative Seating

The child with ASD who has sensory integration dysfunction may need accommodations when it comes to seating because he needs extra sensory input in order to focus. Offer some of these adjustments and alternatives to traditional seating. Classmates often consider special seating a treat, so also let them occasionally choose alternative seating to help make it part of the normal classroom routine.

- **Adjust the chair and desk for optimal posture.** The child's feet should be on the floor (not swinging, which forces the child to balance all of the time), and her upper body should be relaxed—neither hunched nor stooping. A chair with the desk attached may be appropriate as long as it is at the appropriate height.

- **Consult the child's occupational therapist about different types of chair cushions** (beaded, soft, seat and back versus seat only, inflated pillow to allow movement, etc.) that can help the child receive appropriate sensory input, which in turn may encourage him to sit in his chair properly.

- **Have the child sit something other than a chair** such as a therapy ball, T-stool, beanbag chair, or rocking chair to improve muscle tone, especially when she has to sit for long periods. A captain's chair or office chair can provide stability, security, and personal space awareness (because of the chair arms), as well as additional sensory input since the child can spin.

- **Have the child sit backwards on a chair** so that his legs straddle the seat and his chest is up against the back of the chair.

- **Wrap a bungee cord or therapy band around the front legs of the chair for the child to push against or rest her feet on.**

- **Cover a chair with cotton fabric, lambskin, or other textured material for tactile and proprioceptive input.** You can also place sandpaper, a bath mat, different densities of rugs, or a beaded car seat cover under the child's bare feet.

- **The child with ASD does not have to sit at a desk during work periods.** Some may prefer to stand up at a high table or easel; others do their best thinking stretched out on the floor, and still others can't concentrate unless they are in motion. Allow the child to stand at the board, kneel, or lie down when engaged in fine motor tasks, as long as it does not compromise the quality of her work.

Sensory Break Area

The child with ASD needs a place in the classroom in which she can move freely and where she can get away from the high levels of stimulation around her. This area is helpful when she is transitioning from one activity to another or when she demonstrates anxiety or exhibits behaviors that have a foundation in sensory integration dysfunction (rocking, wringing hands, etc.). Use the area to provide a sensory break and, when she is engaging in activities such as reading that do not require the desktop, or to give her a chance to rest her muscles. This area can also be used as an alternative instruction area when large group instruction is too distracting.

- The sensory break area should be away from large group instruction areas.

- It should be relatively free from distractions, such as visual materials, outside noise, high traffic, extreme temperatures, and strong odors.

- The quiet area should contain at least one beanbag chair, cushion, or blanket that will allow the child to sit in a relaxed posture.

- It may contain some soothing materials (play dough, sand and containers for pouring, books, Bubble Wrap®, etc.) that help the child release stress.

- Finally, it should be large enough for the child to have room to move.

Classroom Management

Classroom management refers to organizational, disciplinary, or structural methods you use to maintain order in the classroom. Paying special attention to how you run the classroom can make a huge difference to the child with ASD. Any child can negatively impact the classroom atmosphere if nothing is done to counteract the child's difficulties with attention, organization, time, and social interaction. Manage these problems by adjusting the environment to help prevent the child from becoming a disruptive influence. The child has the best chance to access the curriculum in a carefully controlled atmosphere.

- **Children with ASD may invade others' space or be threatened when someone enters theirs.** Define personal space by placing tape, carpet squares, or plastic hoops on the floor, both around desks and where children gather on the floor.

- **Maintain consistency in morning routines.** For example, each day have the child hang her jacket, unpack her backpack, put her snack in her desk, and then sit in the large group circle. (The picture schedule mentioned on page 19 can be used for this.)

- **Expand the use of the picture schedule** so that the child knows what is coming next and try to maintain a calm routine for the child.

- **Teach how to use specific materials** such as scissors, paintbrushes, or other special materials available only after giving directions for using them.

- **Keep directions short, direct, and simple.**

- **Have children put away equipment at the conclusion of each activity.** This gives closure and helps them transition to the next activity.

- **Provide opportunities for children to use rhythm, music, and other sensory-motor activities as well as for free-play.** Employ short periods of intense movement and alternate with quiet activities. This helps children develop their body images and allows them to refocus.

- **Minimize any incidental light touching** by peers when walking outside the classroom by having the child with ASD be the "engine" or "caboose."

- **Draw a map of the school and laminate it.** Allow the child to use a wipe-off marker to indicate where he is going next.

Transitions

Transitions can be difficult for children with ASD. Show the child how to transition from one activity or location to another. As you get to know the child and understand his processing abilities, plan ahead for the time needed before and during transitions and have a consistent protocol in place to avoid escalating behaviors. Consider using some of these ideas to make changing from one activity to another less traumatic.

- Deliver instruction in short segments. Alternate with free time and movement.

- Collaborate with other teachers when routines are going to change for the students.

- Use peers as role models during transitions like going to recess or lunch.

- Use visual, auditory, and verbal cues to signal transitions.

- Move the child to another desk or table as activities change.

- A picture schedule or other visuals can assist the child during transition times.

- If the child is uncomfortable with transitions, consider using a timer to assist her. A ringing bell is somehow less subjective than a person saying, "OK, time is up."

Timing and Introduction

How you first introduce the child to the classroom is important. Children who feel prepared for the start of the new school year will be more comfortable and are less likely to act out through stress. If possible, meet the child on "his turf" before he visits the classroom. Arrange to meet him at his home or in another familiar environment.

Next, arrange to have him tour the classroom without others in the room. Identify important places, like where supplies go and where different activities take place. Show the materials or the pictures of them that you have put in the area (visual learners) and let them touch the materials or even use them (kinesthetic learners). If you allow the child to select his desk, do this without other children in the classroom to get the clearest picture of where he is comfortable. Reevaluate this choice after other children are in the room and place peers who are good role models near the child with ASD. (For more about peer relationships, see "Facilitating Socialization and Communication" on page 43.)

Teaching Style

If your style of teaching matches the learning styles of all of the children in your classroom, you have hit a home run. However, if your teaching style does not match all children's abilities, including the child with ASD, be open to meeting their needs. Differentiating instruction is critical, and so is differentiating how you deal with each child to make his learning experience excellent.

Be a Calming Influence

Keep your tone calm and even when you are instructing and working with the child with ASD. To help yourself remain calm, expect the unexpected. Consult the child's OT about how to handle certain situations, such as acting out. As these crop up, make adjustments as needed to prevent them. (See "Beyond the Sensory Diet: Behavior Modification" on page 51 for specifics about how to do this.)

To foster self-esteem, verbally praise the child as much as possible, even when only a little progress has been achieved. Do not give false praise, but show that you appreciate effort and a good attitude. Regularly expressing this appreciation will remind you that the child may be giving his best effort at the time. It will also help the child feel good about himself, which can be difficult, especially for high-functioning children on the autism spectrum who are often keenly aware that they are different from their peers.

Finally, note that adult conversations should not occur when you are working closely with children with ASD (or with other children). They are trying to process information all day and adult conversations can confuse or upset them.

Assess Your Instructional Methods

In order to differentiate instruction to the developmental and present level of performance of the child with ASD, you will need to assess pace, size of the instructional group, and how you deliver directions. These changes do not modify the curriculum; rather, they are accommodations that make things easier for the child with ASD and allow her flexibility in absorbing instruction. While these changes will not actually happen until after the child enters the classroom, it helps to think about them beforehand so that you are not adjusting "on the fly."

As you modify your instruction, remember to provide additional support and structure only as needed. Doing more than necessary can impede the student's ability to develop independent skills. And do not hesitate, if it seems appropriate, to extend some of these changes to the child's classmates. Some of these activities will be beneficial for all children (and you are probably already doing them, anyway).

Information and Directions

As you make these adjustments, be sure that each activity is helping the child attain the IEP goals and objectives. Collaborate with special educators and curriculum leaders to make this task manageable. If you must teach curriculum in a manner that is not appropriate for the child, then he should be given alternate tasks. For example, if you have to teach a unit on how to fill out and take a standardized test and it is not on the child's IEP, plan a more appropriate activity. However, don't forget to be creative. Teaching children to properly print their names on their test sheets and to completely fill in bubbles without making stray marks are both important fine motor and writing skills. The child with ASD may not take the test, but chances are that the goals set for him include improving fine motor skills and learning to print his name.

1. Consult the occupational therapist about specific ways to use deep (firm) pressure instead of light touch when it is necessary to move the child or to assist her in an activity.

2. When possible, use smaller group instruction instead of whole class instruction. (Try to do even more of this than you already do.)

3. When introducing new material, begin with individual activities and work toward more cooperative experiences—dual activities to small groups and then to large groups. This will give the child a chance to partially master the material before adding the challenge of socializing.

4. Assess the child's ability to process the language used during classroom instruction. Modify and adjust this language as necessary or take extra time to teach the child the language you are using. This includes curriculum-related vocabulary but also includes showing the child what you mean when you say things like, "Pencils down." A paraprofessional can prompt the child if needed.

5. Adjust the rate at which information is delivered in the classroom to meet the needs of the child with ASD. For example, break long instructional sets into smaller units, delivered as children complete each step.

6. Keep directions clear and concise.

7. Present directions in more than one modality to help meet all children's learning styles. For example, provide written directions to supplement verbal directions, have visuals available when providing verbal information, or give directions in both written and picture form.

8. When you provide multiple modes of instruction, present one mode at a time. For example, if you are speaking, try not to demonstrate until you have finished speaking. Then, tell children to watch as you demonstrate without speaking. Some children with ASD cannot process visual and auditory input concurrently; they can look at you *or* they can be aware of what you are saying. The fact that the child is not looking at you does not mean that he is not listening or attending.

9. Provide concrete, hands-on experiences before teaching abstract information.

10. When appropriate, require the child to indicate comprehension by verbally responding to instruction or directions.

11. Allow for some wait time for the child to answer questions (due to delays in processing information).

12. Allow different methods for the child to produce an assignment. A nonverbal child may be able to draw or point to pictures instead of writing answers.

13. Reduce time spent copying for the child with ASD. For example, provide a worksheet of math problems instead of having the child copy the problems.

14. Provide templates and examples of finished work to assist the child in completing a desired activity, especially with longer or more complex assignments.

15. Shorten assignments or divide them into smaller, more manageable units.

16. Have no time limits for classroom activities to be completed. Let the child put unfinished work aside and complete it in a quiet area at a later time so that he can continue to participate in classroom activities. (If an assignment takes too long, it may not be developmentally appropriate and should be adjusted.)

17. Collect data on the length of time the child can attend. From that point, build on more time gradually until the child can attend for longer periods.

18. Reduce the length requirements on written tasks. Stress quality over quantity.

19. Build on learned information before new information is presented.

20. Until the child learns how to understand the inferences of activities, all activity objectives need to be described to the child in concrete terms. For example, instead of telling the child, "This will help you learn to count to 20," say, "I want you to count how many elephants are on this page."

21. Limit the number of concepts presented at one time.

22. Make assignments meaningful to the child with ASD. For example, the child may be a tactile learner and have difficulty with math worksheets. Instead of using the worksheet, allow her to count manipulatives to complete the problems.

23. Be consistent in following routines as material is delivered.

24. Use the interests and strengths of the child as a motivator. For example, if the child loves to draw and color, have the child color a number of objects and count them for a math assignment. Consult parents and the OT for ideas about what motivates the child.

25. Do not forget to send the child to the sensory break area to complete assignments if the stimulation within the room is too much for the child to process.

Accommodating and Modifying Materials

Remember that *accommodating* means teaching the same content but using different methods, while *modifying* means actually changing content. You may need to adjust curriculum materials to make them developmentally appropriate and match IEP goals. Get help from paraprofessionals and educational trainers and try to do this ahead of time so that the adjustments are made thoughtfully.

General Accommodations

- Highlight or underline instructions and key information on all worksheets.

- Reduce visual noise on worksheets. For example, create a white paper "frame" and copy the worksheet with the frame over it to cover the decorative border.

- Fold papers in half or fourths so that only the items to be worked on are in the child's visual field.

- Match the size of writing or drawing paper to the child's needs. She may need larger paper to express herself in drawings or smaller paper if a large sheet is overwhelming.

- Provide visual and tactile materials in addition to auditory instructions. For example, if you are teaching new vocabulary, say the new words, write them on the board, and provide pictures or actual examples of the items the words name. Or, use manipulatives as you demonstrate math problems and write the numerals on the board.

General Modifications

- If you need to modify content for the child, try to do so in a subtle way. For example, if classmates are doing subtraction with regrouping and this is not appropriate for the child with ASD, cut the problems out of the worksheet and use the rest of the original as a frame. Create problems appropriate for the child with ASD and paste them onto the modified original. After you copy it, the student will have a worksheet that looks like everyone else's, but he can do work at his own level.

- You can also reduce the number of items the student is required to complete or produce. For example, you might simply cover every other problem on the worksheet or assignment and make a copy for the child with ASD, changing reference numbers if necessary.

Accommodations for Specific Curriculum Areas

One way to plan developmentally appropriate, curriculum-based activities that meet the goals and objectives on the IEP is to build a bridge between the areas using special classes (physical education, music, and art) and classroom centers. (If you do not use centers, the supplies for the activities listed on pages 27–31 are inexpensive and readily available.) Effective planning can provide motivating and interesting learning experiences that are within the scope of an IEP and that are helpful for all children in the classroom, but these experiences are especially helpful for children with ASD because they are hands-on and reinforce visual learning. Before using the activities, evaluate whether they help satisfy the goals and objectives of the child's IEP as written and decide whether you should modify them in any way.

Language Arts

- Have children use blocks or other materials to build structures, name them, and make signs identifying each building.

- Ask parents to send in shopping lists or recipes. Have children look in the kitchen area for items on the lists and recipes.

- Reinforce vocabulary and conversation. As children play with toys, encourage them to describe what they are doing and to explain how each toy works.

- Have children describe their art projects as you write down their descriptions.

- Let children use sidewalk chalk to draw shapes, letters, and numbers on the sidewalks. If street signs are visible, have children copy the words.

- Fill a sand and water table (or a shallow, plastic bin) with sand. Have children draw lines and shapes and write numbers and names or vocabulary words in the sand.

- Fill the sand and water table with water and different containers. Ask questions such as, "How full? How much water?"

- Have the child with ASD act out a story he has heard or read aloud.

- Have children dance to music. Then, ask them to describe their movements.

Mathematics

- Have children go outdoors to collect leaves, rocks, and sticks. Have the children count, sort, and group them.

- Let children use software that addresses patterns, grouping, and sorting.

- Help children compare units on measuring cups and spoons.

- Play marching music and have children count out the beats as they march.

- Have children read aloud books with patterns, sizes, counting, or shapes. Provide manipulatives so that children can experience the concepts.

- Provide clay and cookie cutters in the form of basic shapes. Have children identify the shapes they cut out.

- Use toys as manipulatives. Have children describe how many, what size, and what order, and then try to place the toys into a pattern.

- Use the household area for counting. Have children press the numbers on a toy phone in order, count items on a shopping list, sort household items into groups (dairy, meat, and produce), or count silverware or plates.

- During clean-up time, ask children to sort blocks by groups of five, by size, by color, or into other categories.

Science

- Demonstrate how balls and marbles move faster when rolled down ramps.

- In the household area, talk about the functions of different items.

- Have children describe the properties (size, color, texture, weight, and shape) of toys.

- During art time, have children describe tactile properties of paint, clay, and chalk. Ask questions such as, "How does this feel? Is it wet? Sticky? Dusty? Squishy?"

- Mix water with sand or cornstarch. Let children describe the mixture's properties.

- Provide books describing experiments and inventions, as well as how-to books. Follow up with discussion and try doing some of the experiments and projects.

- Play musical instruments. Talk about which instrument makes which sound and how the sounds are made.

- During snack, have children describe the textures, smells, and tastes of their food.

Social Studies

- Take a walk outside. Then, have children use paper and crayons to draw a map.

- In the sand and water table, create rivers, oceans, lakes, roads, mountains, and deserts. Have the children describe where these geographical features may exist.

- Let children explore age-appropriate Web sites about class topics.

- Provide puzzles that correlate to the themes of current social studies units to give children a visual and tactile learning experience.

- Have children describe favorite family recipes: how they taste, where the recipes came from (especially if they are ethnic foods), and how difficult they are to make.

- Research and teach simple dances from different cultures. Talk about how the dances are different from each other and what countries they came from.

- Provide books about children from different cultures. Follow up with a discussion about how we are all different and alike.

- Supply dress-up clothing: uniforms, everyday clothing, and even costumes. As children dress up, discuss where and why they might wear these clothes.

- Provide multicultural people blocks or dolls.

A Special Note about Writing

For most children, writing is crucial to doing well in school. Learning to write takes a special combination of sensorimotor and fine motor skills, visual-perceptual skills, language skills, and cognitive abilities. Because children with ASD often have sensory integration dysfunction, the child's writing ability needs to be carefully assessed by the IEP team. The PT and OT should look at the sensory aspects of writing. A speech and language pathologist should assess vocabulary, auditory discrimination, and syntax/grammar. After assessment, the team can plan appropriate, specific interventions that support graphomotor and cognitive abilities that the child needs to acquire.

Here are some basics that need to be in place as the child engages in the writing process. These may need to be taught separately before "whole" writing is attempted.

- The height of the child's desk and chair must be correct; the child's feet should be flat on the floor and the upper body should be relaxed as he uses the desktop.

- Clear the desk of clutter so that the child can correctly position her paper. Also, place desks far enough apart so that clutter does not "travel" from desk to desk.

- Teach correct paper positioning. Right-handers should rotate the paper 30–35 degrees to the right. Orient the front, left edge of the paper in front of the child's belly button. (Use the opposite position for left-handed children.) Use masking tape on the desktop to create a "picture frame" for papers.

- Provide a variety of implements for coloring, drawing, and writing. Try to match implements to the graphomotor skills of the child and the type of tactile feedback needed. For example, some sizes and shapes of pencils and crayons are a better fit than others. And, some children benefit from the friction provided by a pencil or crayon on paper, while markers provide very little "feedback."

- Thumb and finger location on writing tools is critical and should be monitored on a regular basis. Writing is a motor act, and just as athletes practice each day, children need to practice daily to develop muscle memory for writing.

- Provide the best paper size for the child. If the paper is too small it may keep the child's hand from flowing across the paper and may restrict her ability to express her ideas. If the paper is too large, it may create organizational and motor planning problems. If school policy or curriculum requires the use of grade-level paper, then the IEP must include the alternate size as an accommodation. Also, have the IEP team evaluate and note the appropriate spacing for writing lines on the paper and discuss whether these lines should be standard, raised, darker or lighter, or even absent, depending on the child.

Many children with ASD have dysgraphia (a learning disability that causes difficulty in expressing thoughts in writing) that appears as extremely poor handwriting. Here are activities that offer the necessary proprioceptive input to improve graphomotor skills:

- Engage children in gross motor activities before they write. Let them do crab walks, bear walks, and wheelbarrow walks.

- Have individuals or small groups lie on the floor and move their bodies to create letters and numbers.

- Use jump ropes on the floor to create letters and numbers for children to walk on.

- Put materials slightly out of reach so that the child must reach across the desk or table, crossing the midline of his body to retrieve them with the opposite hand.

- Have children perform simple exercises before writing, such as pushing palms together, pushing down on a desktop, and squeezing and relaxing fists.

- Let children practice screwing and unscrewing jar lids to improve hand strength.

- Have the child tear paper and crumple it. Then, glue the crumpled pieces into the shapes of letters and numbers.

- Let the child build hand strength by using a hole puncher to punch out letters, numbers, and shapes in cardboard. Then, let the child lace the holes with yarn.

- Have the child attempt to peel an orange to facilitate the pincer grasp.

- Teach finger plays, especially those that require pinching fingers together or moving one finger at a time.

- Have children string beads or other objects. (Combine the stringing activity with a math lesson by having the child count the beads or objects and use them to make a pattern.)

- Have children turn over cards, coins, checkers, or buttons without bringing them to the edge of the table.

- Supply coins for children to sort, stack, and put in piggy banks.

- Let children use paper clips or binder clips to attach papers together.

- Provide a box with a lock and several different keys. Fill the box with treats. Let children try the different keys until they can open the box.

- Provide alphabet puzzles and puzzles of individual letters and numbers.

- Build with Lego® bricks or other connecting blocks.

- Let children sort, match, and count small objects into egg cartons.

- Have the children use their index fingers to trace letters and numbers on each other's backs.

- Finger paint letters and numbers, both on a horizontal surface and on an easel. (Vertical surfaces enhance the correct hand position for the child to transfer to the desktop.)

- "Paint" letters on the chalkboard with water and paintbrushes or with spray bottles filled with water and set to "stream." (Also, use a spray bottle to water plants.)

- Have children paint numbers or pictures with square pieces of sponge and paint.

- Write letters and numbers in sand, shaving cream, cornmeal, rice, etc.

- Create letters/numbers by gluing small pasta shapes or beans on cardboard surfaces or by cutting out textured material like sandpaper, fabric, or plastic. (You can also glue different materials to cutout letters to create textured letters or use the glue itself to make letters and then let it dry.) Have the child with ASD repeatedly trace the letters and numbers with his finger to build understanding of them. Use the cutouts as manipulatives.

- Outline letters and numbers with push pins. Have the child wind yarn around the push pins to create dot-to-dot patterns.

- Use clay and play dough to form letters and numbers. Then, "erase" the characters with a rolling pin (for extra sensory input). Eventually, build only parts of the letters so that the child must complete them.

- Draw letters and numbers in clay with chopsticks or let children build letters by pushing toothpicks into a flattened bed of clay.

- Let children use medicine droppers and colored water to write on colored paper.

- Give children small pieces of sidewalk chalk (no longer than 1" (2.54cm) to facilitate the tripod grip) and let them write on chalkboards or outside on sidewalks.

- Build letters and numbers with craft sticks, chopsticks, and yarn soaked in starch.

- Provide large magnetic letters and numbers on a vertical surface. Or, scatter the magnets on the floor. Build a fishing rod from a dowel, string, and a paper clip, and let the child fish for and identify the letters he catches.

- Let children form letters using masking tape.

- Provide small, resealable plastic bags in which to store items. (Children use the pincer grip to close the bags.)

- Create patterns with colored clothespins for children to continue or copy or let them use the clothespins to pick up letter tiles as they identify the letters.

- Slip a pencil through the holes of a hollow, plastic golf ball. Have the child hold the ball while writing.

- Have the child hold cotton balls, gummy candy, or other small, soft items in the palm of his hand while writing.

- Teach sign language for fine motor skills. The letters *d, f,* and *o* create the web space in the hand that is optimal for writing.

- Eat snacks with chopsticks. (Stop if children find this frustrating rather than fun.)

- Let children search for the letters in their names in magazines or newspapers.

Just reading many of the suggested changes from this chapter on the IEP can seem daunting and the task of implementing them even more so. Make sure you ask for (and get) the support you need from other professionals to make these changes and record them on the IEP as needed. Remember, too, that the changes will often benefit all of the children in your classroom, not just the child with ASD.

Finally, as you continue to adjust the classroom and your teaching methods through the school year, also continue to strive to meet the needs of the child with ASD, even if it seems that progress is not being made. Children with ASD need repetition, continuity, experience, and significant amounts of time to improve. If you offer these, and remember to measure the child's progress against her IEP goals, you will be much more satisfied than if you measure her against unrealistic goals.

Chapter Five
Available to Learn:
Providing Appropriate Sensory Input

Perhaps the most challenging part of integrating a child with ASD into a regular classroom is managing behaviors. This chapter explains what most researchers feel are the origins of the group of behaviors commonly associated with ASD, and strategies for managing them. By reading this chapter, planning ahead with the IEP team (especially the OT and PT), and getting to know the child, hopefully you will understand the reasons behind some behaviors and help the child replace them with more appropriate ones.

Sensory Integration Issues and Being Available to Learn

Children with ASD usually have sensory processing issues. They often must direct so much cognitive and emotional energy to negotiating sensory input that they may not have enough energy left to sit still, much less be "available to learn." Being "available to learn" simply means that a child is free from distractions and can absorb new learning. Children with ASD may have so many special sensory needs that they may spend all of their time meeting those needs. For this reason, many require special therapy based on regulating their sensory integration—a term for how the brain processes, organizes, and interprets sensory input.

The Sensory Systems

In addition to the more familiar visual and auditory systems, there are also tactile, vestibular, and proprioceptive systems. **Tactile system** information (received through the skin) helps us learn about the quality of objects and our bodies. Touch is a basic component in motor planning because it detects pain, temperature, and pressure—important information that ensures protection of inner organs, muscles, and bones. Input from the **vestibular system** is received from the inner ear and is activated by movement or by changing head position. This system works with the visual system to form a sense of self, position in the environment, and coordination. This system governs movement, balance, and equilibrium. Sensory information from the **proprioceptive system** is received through the joints, muscles, and tendons. It provides awareness about our body parts and allows us to perform tasks with coordination. This system maintains joint stability, detects pressure (both felt and applied), and determines how much pressure to use for things like maintaining posture, holding objects, and planning and coordinating motor tasks. Together, these systems organize sensory input and help us function well.

The child with ASD is often unable to register, organize, process, and interpret sensations and has trouble coordinating them with vision and hearing, which leads to sensory integration dysfunction. These children often have hypoactive or hyperactive sensory systems or combinations of the two that vary from day to day. Those with hypoactive systems seek additional stimulation, while those with hyperactive sensory systems avoid it. Many children with ASD register sensations inconsistently because while they react to the changing environment like everyone else, they are less able to adapt to these changes.

Typical Behaviors That Result from Sensory Integration Dysfunction

A child with ASD who has sensory integration dysfunction may:

- Be unresponsive to sensory stimulation. For example, he may not seem to feel pain or hear loud noises.

- Show abnormal awareness and concentration. For example, she does not acknowledge conversation or make eye contact but can focus on a spinning record for hours.

- Have difficulty regulating his activity level. During quiet activities, the child may crave more stimulation and create it with rocking or humming. During noisy activities, the child may feel threatened and retreat or become tactile defensive.

- Engage in perseveration (repetitive behavior such as rocking, pacing, wringing or flapping hands, chewing on clothing or objects, humming), and echolalia (repeating words and phrases). Perseveration can also be a preoccupation with something the child likes, such as watching a snippet of a video for hours on end.

- Have a hard time with transitions and changes in routine, perhaps because when she has found an appropriate sensory input level, changing it threatens this equilibrium.

- Overreact to sensory input or new situations, and thus feel so anxious that she has a fight/flight/fright response and may resort to biting, scratching, running away, or self-inflicting an injury.

- Show a deficit in fine and gross motor skills.

- Have poor body awareness and recognition of body parts and their functions.

- Attempt to regulate sensory information through oral motor activities such as licking lips or grinding teeth together.

- Have trouble deciphering odors and distinguishing tastes.

- Have impaired speech and a limited establishment of language due to auditory deficits (auditory system).

- Take a long time to establish even a poor visual percept (visual system).

- Be overly sensitive to textures; for example, he may resist solid food because of the consistency (tactile system).

- React negatively to tight touch but respond better to deep pressure—touch that is firm enough to be felt under the skin (tactile system).

- Not react to falling or hurting himself unless it is very intense (tactile system).

- Resist normal movement, such as climbing stairs or jumping and be gravitationally insecure, afraid of losing balance where others would not be (vestibular system).

- Seek large quantities of sensations like whirling, rocking, or fluttering the fingers in the peripheral visual field (vestibular system).

- Have trouble forming a clear perception of his body and its relationship to space and the environment (proprioceptive system).

- Have trouble interacting with other people because he is not sure how he relates to them in space (proprioceptive system).

- Be clumsy or have an unusual posture or gait (proprioceptive system).

A deficit in the proprioceptive system can combine with other system deficits to produce dyspraxia (poor motor planning—a poor ability to organize, plan, and execute new and unpracticed motor tasks). Poor motor planning frequently challenges children with ASD. Poor sensory processing hinders the development of motor planning capacity from many angles. The child often cannot readily form a visual percept of an object in front of him and may have trouble abstracting the potential use of an object. He may be reluctant to engage in purposeful activity and may also resist doing anything new and different. When he does do new things, it may not be pleasurable to him. When presented with the need for a new, unlearned response, he cannot put together a coordinated action. The child's motor activity may also be influenced by poor modulation of sensation arising from gravitational insecurity, which will certainly give rise to unpleasant sensations unless the environment is set up for his success. Finally, if he cannot modulate the vestibular input, he may make himself immobile.

Motor planning is required for visual tracking, pointing to objects, and learning signs, and it depends on knowing about the functions of body parts and how they move. The child with ASD who cannot perceive his physical environment well or act effectively upon it lacks the basic material for organizing more complex behaviors.

The underlying cause of sensory integration dysfunction is unclear. Our brains "decide" which sensory input to bring to our attention and whether we should do something about it. Research shows that this part of the brain is not working well in the child with ASD, so he may not register things that everyone else notices, or he may over-register one sensation and under-register another—his brain has a hard time knowing which information is important. He may stare through people, avoid eye contact, or pay no attention to objects and toys. Yet, sometimes his brain will decide to give careful, prolonged attention to some tiny detail, such as lines on the floor. This may be why so many children with ASD either crave vigorous movement and vestibular stimulation, or reject it entirely. Neither response is normal, but satisfying this craving may help the brain process other sensory input, especially visual input.

As a result of not being able to process sensory input, many "typical" autistic behaviors are caused by the child's need to regulate body functions and cope with the environment. In order for children with ASD who have sensory integration dysfunction to succeed in a changing environment like a classroom, their sensory systems need to be stabilized. Modulation—the brain's regulation of its own activity—involves facilitating some neuronal messages to produce more of a perception or response, and inhibiting other messages to reduce extraneous input. Simply put, the child's brain must be retrained to pay more attention to things like people and toys and also to ignore the lines on the floor.

This is a long explanation of how it may feel to have ASD, but it is important. Imagine trying to learn the rules of a game when the game changes every time you play. Understanding what a child with ASD faces in order to do simple things like sit still, acknowledge that someone is talking to her, and absorb instruction can make a big difference in your attitude toward this child. It helps to realize that the child's problem is not a behavioral one, but a physical one that involves the action of electrical impulses and chemicals in the brain. A learning disorder or behavior problem resulting from brain dysfunction is just as much of a physical difficulty as a broken leg.

It also helps to recognize that a child with ASD has a less stable nervous system than those of other children. Too much stimulation (movement, people, confusion, changes in schedule, noise, visual noise, demands, or light touch) can cause him to lose control of his emotions because he cannot regulate them—his brain is too busy elsewhere. You and the IEP team should try to gauge the amount of auditory and visual stimulation that the child is capable of processing and then try to match these levels in the LRE (whether this means lesser *or* greater levels of stimulation). Together you can discuss appropriate accommodations and modifications that help the child remain stable and available to learn.

Eliminating these behaviors entirely may be impossible, as they are needed for the child to function. However, these behaviors can often be managed—reduced to a low level or replaced by other, more appropriate behaviors that serve the same purpose. There are two approaches to assisting the child with ASD to make sense of the sensory world. These are 1) keeping the environment very stable from day to day and 2) facilitating the child's ability to process sensory input into meaningful information. You can certainly make some strides toward providing a very stable classroom. However, it is impossible to teach the child in a vacuum, so it seems more useful in the long run to develop his ability to process and organize input so that new situations or sensory input will no longer produce panic, anxiety, anger, or inappropriate behaviors. The IEP team should plan for options in both areas, depending on what is appropriate for the child. Finally, remember that each child with ASD is different, and what works for some may not work for others or may not work every day with the same child.

Providing a More Stable Environment

Undesirable behaviors in a child with ASD will increase when she is under stress. Structure and consistency in the environment lower stress and promote good organization of the brain, which leaves her more available to learn. General suggestions for preserving a stable environment (detailed in the chapter titled "The Learning Environment: Adjusting the Classroom and the Curriculum" on page 15) include eliminating contact with objects that produce negative reactions; using headphones, earmuffs, or earplugs to limit auditory stimulation; helping classmates respect her personal space; eliminating visual noise; maintaining a consistent, predictable schedule; sending her to the area designated for sensory breaks; and asking parents to provide a variety of toys for the sensory break area that comfort the child. Beyond these general suggestions, the IEP team should research whether a sensory diet could help the child function better.

The Purpose of a Sensory Diet

A child with ASD who frequently resorts to his own methods of coping with sensory input may benefit from a daily "sensory diet" of tactile, vestibular, and proprioceptive activities monitored by an OT. These activities should act as a small break and diminish the need for unacceptable behavior. Some activities, like rocking, may be ones that the child engages in already, but when used as part of a preplanned sensory diet, they become part of the class routine rather than a disruption. For example, if classmates understand that, every day, Susanne needs to go to the sensory break area and rock before math time, it is far less disruptive for them—and for Suzanne—than if she gets overloaded and wails until someone figures out that she needs to go to the rocking chair. When carefully chosen and used on a regular basis (preferably when a child needs it and not on a schedule, although the child may enjoy the predictability of a schedule), a sensory diet can develop changes in the nervous system that helps her regulate sensory input and become a functioning participant in the classroom. The sensory diet plan should also be used at home. Teach parents to use the diet to enhance the child's progress.

Creating the Sensory Diet

Sensory diet activities fall into three categories: calming, alerting, or organizing (a combination of both calming and alerting). Calming activities are helpful when the child with ASD is overwhelmed, when he is transitioning, or when there is noise or movement in the room. Examples include oral motor activities (sucking hard candies or drinking a milk shake through a straw); engaging in slow, rhythmic movement (rocking or swinging); wrapping a blanket around the shoulders; and pushing against walls with the body.

Alerting activities help the child refocus when he seems unable to pay attention. They can give him the sensory input his brain craves so that he can move beyond the need and return his attention to the task at hand. They can also prepare him for transitions. Alerting activities include light touch; light tickles (with a feather, back scratcher, or Koosh® ball); fast, irregular movement (bouncing on a therapy ball, playing tag, or jumping); and eating crunchy foods (pretzels, crackers, popcorn, or raw vegetable sticks).

Organizing activities can be both alerting and calming. They help the child regulate his responses to sensory input. Activities include pushing and pulling (playing with a stretchy toy or stiff clay or pushing a loaded cart); moving furniture; putting away chairs; hiking; tug-of-war; carrying and passing out books; and eating chewy foods like gum, bagels, fruit bars, and dried fruit.

You should know the reasons you are choosing certain activities. The OT and IEP team should meet to discuss what activities are appropriate and why, as well as how they should be administered. The OT should train all teachers, parents, and staff to administer the therapy and to monitor results to ensure that the activities are appropriate.

Sensory Diet Implementation

Timing, structure, and how you implement the sensory diet are all important. The IEP team and the OT should determine a trial period for the sensory diet (two weeks, one month, etc.), and establish how to collect data that will show how successful the sensory diet is. (See page 42 for a reproducible Sensory Diet Planning Sheet.)

Next, work with the OT and IEP team to create a list of what activities to use and guidelines for when to use them. Determine which parts of the daily classroom schedule are calming for the child and which are overwhelming; then, plan activities accordingly. Allot developmentally appropriate lengths of time for the child to participate in a sensory activity, even if that time is "as long as the child needs it." You may be able to create a daily schedule for this input by following the child's lead.

As the IEP team plans activities, make the activities as enjoyable as possible. For example, consult parents about ideas for how to motivate the child. If a child likes a certain cartoon, have the child carry a weighted backpack with the cartoon characters on it or trace the letters in the names of the characters or spin or march to the cartoon's theme music. (Rhythmic music to activities makes them more predictable and organizing.)

Next, plan how to best utilize paraprofessionals and the OT and PT in administering some of the sensory input. This is for a variety of reasons. Some deep pressure activities may require too much touching for your comfort level. Some may be disruptive or draw too much attention to the child's differences and should happen outside of the classroom. Some may be very time-consuming. You must maintain the classroom for all students, so delegate where appropriate. Do be certain, though, that the opportunity for sensory activities is present as the child needs it, not based on someone else's availability.

Do not feel you have to limit participation in all sensory activities to the child with ASD. Alternating vigorous and passive activity time can benefit all children. Letting the whole class march on Bubble Wrap® or manipulate clay prior to writing is fun and stimulating for all children, and it will help the child with ASD stand out less from his peers.

Once the sensory diet is in place, carefully monitor the child for any positive or negative effects. If you do not see improvement, work with the IEP team to change the activities, their timing, or duration. Keep trying until you find a plan that works.

Specific Ideas for a Sensory Diet: Tactile Sensory Input
To help a child with ASD that is under- or oversensitive to tactile input or who is tactile defensive, remember to have the child stand in the back of the line and sit in the corner of large groups so that he can determine his personal space. Allow him to choose alternative positions for working: lying on his stomach, sitting on the floor or in a rocking chair or curled up in a corner. Also try the following options (in consultation with the OT and PT).

- Touch with deep pressure instead of light pressure. Gently but firmly squeezing the arm is preferable to gently rubbing or tapping. (Consult the OT and follow guidelines for touching children as set by your school.)

- Allow the child to play in bare feet or march on bubble wrap. Receptors on the soles of the feet signal changes in texture and weight.

- Have the OT roll a large ball over the child while he is lying down.

- Let the child roll and crawl over different textures and shapes (balls, carpet squares, rolled rugs, etc.).

- Let the child wrap himself in sheets, blankets, or beach towels.

- Fill a tactile bin in the classroom with rice, water, gelatin, cornmeal, marshmallows, or any other substance that the child with ASD will enjoy.

- Play discrimination games. Have the child close her eyes, feel for, and guess objects. Bury these objects in sand or rice if desired.

- Play matching games to identify objects with identical textures or weights.

- Have the child manipulate clay prior to a fine motor or writing activity.

- Have the child mix dough and water in a large bowl and then roll it out.

- Have the child stand at a chalkboard with her eyes closed. Guide her hand to write letters or numbers. Then, have her guess what they are.

- Have the child draw letters, numbers, and shapes with finger paint; in flattened clay using a pencil or chop sticks; on a desktop using shaving cream, whipped cream, pudding, cornstarch, or hand cream; on a partner's back with an index finger (the partner should guess the letter); with a wet sponge on a chalkboard; or with a finger, tracing letters on carpet or sandpaper.

- Engage in projects that require gluing.

- Teach finger plays.

- Let the child do some partner activities, such as using soft, dry paintbrushes to pretend to paint themselves and each other, moving to music together, or building letters on the floor. Partner activities encourage tolerance for light touch.

- Offer socially appropriate ways of making physical contact throughout the day, such as shaking hands, patting the child on the back, or giving high fives.

- Have children build human pyramids in groups of three or six.

Specific Ideas for a Sensory Diet: Vestibular and Proprioceptive Input

Children's responses to vestibular input may be just as varied as their responses to tactile input. Some love it; others do not. Rocking in a chair may be as much as one child can tolerate, while another may need much more stimulation. When there is evidence of decreased processing of vestibular and proprioceptive input information, you can try these activities. Because of the disruption factor, for some activities it may be best for the child to leave the room and participate with a paraprofessional, the OT, or PT. Also, see page 20 (Alternative Seating) for additional ideas.

- Consult the OT or PT about having the child wear a weighted vest or backpack (or ankle and wrist weights). Also, allow the child to carry heavy books or help move furniture in the classroom.

- Schedule daily deep pressure exercise: doing push-ups while leaning on a chair or therapy ball, shifting weight from side to side while sitting in a chair or long ways on a bolster, pressing hands together or down on the head, crossing arms and pressing down on the shoulders or up on the elbows, rubbing hands firmly down the arms, pressing on knees, sitting on the hands, rotating shoulders and upper trunk from side to side, tilting the head rhythmically from side to side, or standing with back against a wall and then sliding into a sitting position ("wall sitting").

- Let the class do bear walks, crab walks, mule kicks, frog jumps, bunny hops and wheelbarrow walks when transitioning to another part of the classroom, or let them crawl with beanbags balanced on their backs.

- Use classroom games to practice body part identification, laterality, directionality, listening skills, and crossing midline activities. Consult your physical education teacher for ideas.

- In a separate room, let the child put his hands on the shoulders or hips of the occupational therapist to be led physically so that he receives the kinesthetic feeling of fast, slow, or uneven time by running or walking. (You may want to do this at the beginning of the year when you take the child on a tour of the empty classroom.) Also, lead the child around the classroom to demonstrate distances and spatial relationships within the environment.

- Physically show the child how to be tall, short, wide, or thin. Have him emulate the movements.

- Kneel on the floor, facing the child, or have the class work in pairs. Place the palms of your hands gently against his and then firmly push. Repeat with feet.

- Have the child bend, stretch, twist, turn, march, hop, jump, and shake as many body parts as possible to music.

- Let the child jump on a mini-trampoline.

- Using masking tape, create shapes on the floor. Let children jump into and out of the shapes, jumping forward, backward, and sideways. Children can also jump over ropes, both while they are moving or while lying on the ground.

- Use the outside playground equipment as an additional sensory break area throughout the day. Help the child climb the hanging ropes and cargo net.

- As a class project, let children plant flowers around the school. Allow the child with ASD to dig holes.

- Have the child erase the chalkboards and then wash them with sponges.

- Let the child mop the floor or rake leaves.

- Ask questions or read statements that contain action words such as, *The snake slithered through the grass*. Then, have the class act out the action words.

- Show the child how to move from one place to another by sitting on a scooter board and pushing off with her feet, or using a plunger to "row" herself. She can also lie prone on the scooter board and push off the wall or pull herself along a length of secured rope. Or, have a peer or paraprofessional sit on the scooter and hold a jump rope or hoop so that the child with ASD can pull him along.

- Teach the child to swing in a hammock swing.

- Let children play Follow the Leader or have a tug-of-war.

- When you have the class clean out their desks, let everyone crumple wastepaper into little balls and toss them into a recycling bin.

Specific Ideas for a Sensory Diet: Motor Planning

Each of the following movement experiences can enhance every child's school performance by developing body awareness, body scheme, and space awareness; enhancing attending skills, aural comprehension, and visual perception skills; and developing self-esteem and confidence. Get help from the physical education teacher, OT, and PT to find activities that your class will enjoy.

- Have children march, jump, or skip in a pattern to music with a strong beat.

- Combine movement with academics. For example, have an alphabet relay. Assign children to three or four groups on one side of the classroom. On the other side of the room, gather sets of uppercase letters. When you say, "Go," the first child on each team should crawl across the room, find the A, place it on the floor, and return to her team. Repeat until all teams have completed the alphabet. The first team to finish wins the game.

- Lead a short, vigorous movement activity before children are required to sit for a long time. If the child with ASD cannot sit for very long, use a timer to determine how long he can sit and attend. Plan for short breaks at these time limits.

- Use an accessible outdoor area as a classroom on a regular basis so that children have freedom to move and are able to focus afterward.

- Initiate activities where children's arms and legs cross the midline of their bodies (crawling, running, swinging, or touching opposite toes) to provide bilateral input.

- Have children move their bodies while remaining in the same space, such as by stretching arms or lying on the floor and raising legs. This helps children becomes aware of how the body can move without traveling through space.

- When engaged in locomotor movement (movement through space), children develop an awareness of how the body moves about, understand the language used to describe locomotor movement, develop improved balance when starting and stopping, develop improved movement sequencing (motor planning), and learn to feel comfortable about moving.

- Offer balls, balloons, and beanbags for children to use while moving.

- Allow children plenty of time for free play so that they can move freely and with less structure and fewer verbal cues, and environmental restrictions. Exploring movement creates an arena for the child to learn new ways to move and integrate those movements into motor planning.

Movement activities and language acquisition opportunities can be done simultaneously, thus creating input for all sensory areas. Use the following ideas to help children move and learn:

- Have children follow movement instructions. Children with ASD may find it difficult to follow combinations of spoken, visual, and hands-on directions. Therefore, present more than one type of directions but use only one at a time. After giving directions, ask questions to gauge the child's understanding.

- Improve awareness of body movement and function by having the child talk about movement while doing it, planning and then execute a movement, recall a completed movement, and link a single movement to a single word.

- Help children achieve the difficult task of expressing creativity in nonlocomotor or locomotor movement, both with and without objects, and changing that movement in some way. Use simple problem solving (Can you find a way to get around the chair without walking?), guided exploration (Let's talk about all of the ways we could get around the chair, and then try some.), and imagery (Imagine the chair is a mountain and you are a bird. How would you get around the chair?).

On the following page is a reproducible Sensory Diet Planning Sheet. With the help of the IEP team, fill out the sheet to add activities to the child's day in order to help fulfill her sensory needs. Once the sensory diet is in place, follow up with feedback and observations about what works and what doesn't.

Sensory Diet Planning Sheet

(Directions are found on pages 40–41.)

Child's Name: _____

Sensory Diet Onset Date: _____

Teacher/OT/PT: _____

Sunday	Monday	Tuesday	Wednesday	Thursday	Friday	Saturday

Chapter Six
Facilitating Socialization and Communication

Many children with ASD have social deficits. Areas usually affected include interaction and two-way communication, abstract reasoning, and executive functioning (an umbrella term for things like planning, working memory, controlling impulses, inhibition, mental flexibility, and initiating or monitoring actions). These children have trouble making eye contact; understanding body language, facial expressions, and small talk; completing a group activity or conversation; moving to a new subject; showing empathy (due to their rigid, structured manner); and demonstrating or initiating age-appropriate play and social experiences. Perseveration (the tendency to fixate on a subject or repeat an action) is an additional stumbling block to social development; children with ASD cannot socialize because they are too busy repeating an action or immersing themselves in a subject, or they may linger too long within a theme of a conversation that is uninteresting to others.

In addition to the social deficits listed above, children with ASD often have a variety of speech deficits (due to sensory integration dysfunction) that may be exacerbated by poor intellectual and social development. Speech deficits impact the acquisition of cognitive skills, social skills, and the ability to express wants and needs.

Children with ASD are often concrete learners; they need structure and routine to function. The unpredictability of using language in the social world is challenging, as is developing a sense of self and self-esteem. Fortunately, there are ways to make inroads into their world and bring children with ASD into ours. Using a combination of language activities, motor activities, and cognitive activities will foster focus and concentration, engagement with the external world, and two-way intentional communication for all kinds of learners. The right mix of modalities (beyond using only language) will often create interactive experiences the child can use to develop a sense of self, as well as to learn to reach out to others.

This is an area that can be neglected on a child's IEP. Social skill building is more abstract than curriculum. For the child with ASD, however, it is equally important, if not more so, to build this skill set. Make sure that the IEP team builds in ways for helping the child learn to communicate with you and classmates and learn how to ask for what he needs and wants.

Working "with" Autism to Foster Social Skills

Children with ASD tend to seek out activities that provide sensory experiences most beneficial to them at this point in their development. It is this exploration that helps the child become a more mature, efficient organizer of sensory information and creates opportunities for him to reach out for social interaction. The child seeks sensory input that provides him with a concrete experience. He will begin to understand and generalize abstract concepts through these concrete sensory motor experiences.

The tendency of many IEP teams is to modify, adapt, and seek solutions for only curriculum offerings; however, social development is equally important for children with ASD. IEP teams should plan for social skill development by brainstorming ways to use the child's behaviors and fixations to build and stretch negotiation and communication periods. Teams can adapt the strategies listed on page 44 to the unique characteristics of the child in order to improve socialization and communication skills.

Socialization Strategies

- **If the child perseverates**, make the behavior an interaction so that it is no longer perseverative. For example, if a child loves tracing lines on the gymnasium floor, get on the floor and trace along with him, thus using this connection to build the foundation for higher levels of communication.

- **Some children with ASD demonstrate fixation**—an extreme interest in something—which can be used to motivate them to relate to the external world. For example, if a child is fixated on a certain food, reward him with a taste of the food only when he uses words to ask for it.

- **When trying to break fixations or stop perseveration** can cause children to exhibit impulsive behaviors that will hamper social opportunities. While trying to find appropriate substitutions for these behaviors, expect and plan for some acting out.

- **The IEP team should work with the child, whether she is verbal or nonverbal, to develop a repertoire of cues and prompts to express her needs** (especially in times of high anxiety and frustration) in the most socially appropriate manner possible.

- **Teach the child how to maintain his position in space, how to stand, and how to make and maintain eye contact when engaging in conversation with peers.** If he moves too close or walks away during conversation, it reduces his ability to foster two-way communication. Understanding posture and position in space during a social encounter can assist the child to build future social interactions.

- **Practice the skills needed to maintain the child's presence in a two-way conversation with peers.** During one-to-one interaction and small group experiences, remind her to make eye contact; maintain the proper personal space, position, and posture; take turns; and ask and answer questions.

- **Use pictures of gestures and facial expressions to teach nonverbal communication.** (Research suggests that we communicate nonverbally 93% of the time.)

- **Teach greetings and good-byes verbally** (hi, hello, nice to see you, see you later, good-bye, etc.) **and nonverbally** (shaking hands, giving a "high five," waving, etc.) to provide a foundation for future higher levels of interaction.

- **Replace inappropriate social behaviors with appropriate ones.** Use different modes of learning to demonstrate. For example, if a child is a kinesthetic learner, teach him to raise his hand when he needs something.

- **Developing social stories** told by the social worker or school psychologist can help the child understand the nuances of communication. Read books with social stories as the theme and have the child act out the stories.

- **Acting as a translator, break conversations into smaller segments** so that the child begins to associate finding meaning with the act of having a conversation.

- **Role-play numerous scenarios** for the child to help her begin to understand the nuances of conversation and social cues.

- **Socially inappropriate behaviors may surface during transitions.** Provide practice for experiencing transitions.

- **Teach social skills in nonacademic settings.** Lunch, recess, and other social times offer numerous unstructured, natural opportunities for interaction.

- **If the child does have some expressive language, build on his strengths in this area to lay a foundation for future communication and social interactions.** For example, if a child can sing songs, incorporate favorite songs as well as new ones in the curriculum. Ask the child to lead the singing. Then, discuss the songs afterward to reinforce using the words from the lyrics in conversation.

- **Select opportunities for the child to engage in a high-interest activity that she finds highly motivating.** This activity will create numerous occasions to develop expressive language and learn social cues like taking turns. Build these opportunities throughout the day. If the academic demands dictate that there is not enough time in the day for these activities, have them added to the IEP as a strategy and/or an accommodation.

- **Explore "reverse mainstreaming."** Have the child and his peers work together in social and play experiences in a setting normally used by the child with ASD, such as the resource room or his sensory break area. The quieter area can allow the child with ASD to focus on the subtleties of social experiences.

- **Use peers as role models and "buddies" in large group activities.** Having a buddy work with the child with ASD may provide the template and visual cues to allow him to attend and focus.

As you work on creating a social experience for the child, you should bring data to the IEP team so that they can continually analyze the child's progress, especially in the area of behavior. Many plans have expected behaviors that are too demanding on the child and can actually hinder his learning of appropriate social skills. Continue to ensure that any socialization or behavioral plan is in keeping with the child's developmental abilities.

Dealing with Curious Classmates

Other children in the classroom will probably be curious about their classmate's behavior, especially if he acts out a lot or is very unresponsive. Children will probably ask questions and may need reassurance. The best way to deal with these questions is to be open about the fact that this child is different and explain why and how in terms the children can understand. The following are some responses you can fall back on during these discussions.

Start by explaining that everyone learns differently. In the classroom, you might mention that the child with ASD needs to use the rocking chair to "warm up," just like athletes have to warm up for sports or games. In the same way that he needs to rock, some of them may need to get a drink of water or take off a sweater to be comfortable enough to learn. Next, remind children that they all need adult assistance to learn, and this child needs a little more assistance from you than others.

Try to make other children aware that the child with ASD is communicating in his own way. Say things like, "When he flaps his hands, he may be telling us he is excited about something." "Sometimes, he puts hands over his ears because the sounds in the room seem louder to him than they do to you." If you help classmates understand the cues the child offers, they may start helping you communicate with the child by asking him to show what he is excited about, or lowering their voices to make him more comfortable.

When children ask questions about modifying and adapting curriculum, give examples of how teachers modify and adapt lessons for all children in the classroom so that they have a sense of fairness. Examples are choosing books for children that are on their reading levels, reviewing a math lesson several times, and choosing favorite games for the class to play during recess.

Use this opportunity to raise children's awareness in general. Select stories that describe children with disabilities. Follow up with questions and answers about why some children cannot talk or walk, and why they may act and perform differently. School psychologists and social workers can select social stories and facilitate role-playing, as well as help you plan a diversity day to teach the school about disabilities.

Finally, enlist children as helpers. Explain that your class was selected as a good, safe place for the child with ASD to learn. Make it a reward to be a good role model for this child by letting well-behaved children sit near him at lunch or be his partner when transitioning. Praise classmates when they attempt to include the child with ASD and as they deal with him in a positive manner, but do not go overboard. The child should be treated as a member of the classroom; lavishing too much praise on other children for helping or talking to the child with ASD means treating him more like a special guest than a full-fledged class member. Hopefully, children will learn to be protective and supportive of their classmate with ASD, but still treat him much like any other classmate.

The Effect of ASD on Communication and Language Development

Communication is vital to the child's success with socialization and with school in general. As sensory input constantly bombards the child, a lack of expressive language can cause frustration, anxiety, and a fight or flight response. This practice can snowball into previolent episodes because the child may only be able to express his needs physically (by hitting, kicking, pulling hair, running away, etc.). IEP team members should collaborate on improving language skills with ongoing consultation from the speech and language pathologist. Understanding the child's language level and offering a consistent improvement program are critical for the child's growth.

Communication disorders within the ASD spectrum vary. Verbal children with ASD may possess some communication strengths, including:

- **Rote memorization of facts and figures**, such as days of the week, months, phone numbers, and people's names. The ability to retrieve this information is a strength, but some children perseverate on this information.

- **Episodic memory** (remembering the details of an event very clearly). Episodic memory gives children with ASD a strong connection to the event, which may help them link the meanings of words that were said during it. This can lead to increased language learning, but the strong connection can also make them less flexible. For example, if a child had a fantastic time rolling a truck across the floor while playing with his father, he may later have difficulty using *roll* in other contexts because it is so closely linked to *truck*.

- **Visuospatial processing** (the ability to understand and use the sensory information they receive through their sense of vision). This is why visual cues and prompts are so often useful in aiding the child's understanding and use of language.

- **Rule-based information processing.** If the rules are very concrete, then the child with ASD can often follow and remember them.

- **Gestalt processing:** Children with ASD often hear and process whole sentences, but have trouble picking out specific words from those sentences.

- **The ability to recognize patterns quite easily.** This can lead to good categorization skills and early reading ability.

Children with ASD often possess deficits, including:

- **Joint attention**—the ability to "coordinate attention between interactive social partners with respect to objects or events in order to share an awareness of the objects or events" (Mundy et al., 1986, p. 657). Joint attention behaviors include sharing attention (through the use of alternating gaze or pointing) and following or directing the attention of another. Essentially, it is the propensity of a child to engage another's attention to share enjoyment of objects or events; children both initiate and respond to joint attention bids. Research suggests that joint attention skills are markedly impaired in children with ASD and that joint attention plays a critical role in the development of language and play skills. Children with better joint attention skills tend to exhibit improved outcomes in a number of areas of development, and studies suggest that it is possible to improve these skills in children with ASD. Therefore, targeting joint attention development appears to be an important component of early intervention.

- **Social orienting**—the ability to understand social cues (such as turning to look at another child while conversing). A child with ASD may show no nonverbal signs that he is aware of another communication partner.

- **The ability to monitor emotional states.** This means understanding and processing social cues in order to respond to the conversation with the appropriate emotions. Children with ASD tend to be less aware of the emotional states of peers. They may not smile when the peer is doing something interesting or if an exciting surprise happens in the class. They fail to realize when their communication partner is bored or does not understand them.

- **Considering another's intentions.** They may not notice or understand the nonverbal communication that the communication partner is using. These children may not realize when they are being insensitive to others.

- **Social reciprocity.** Children with ASD have trouble initiating interaction and may fail to learn how to initiate, engage in, and terminate conversations. They have trouble taking turns, responding to cues to continue or end conversations, and recognizing humor and shifts in conversation themes. They may not allow others to finish their thoughts during conversations.

Children with ASD also have trouble with language and related cognitive skills, as in the following examples:

- **Children with ASD can fail to understand and use symbolic language.** They respond inconsistently to auditory input and may not hear individual words.

- **Auditory attention** and **auditory memory** produce difficulties in comprehension, such as hearing "the whole but not the parts," longer processing time, and trouble using their hearing when they are using other senses.

- **Complex sentence structure**, which limits their ability to communicate about past and future events, to clarify cause-and-effect relationships, and to give background information may cause problems for children with ASD.

- **Semantics** (interpretation of words, signs, sentences, idioms, metaphors, similes, ironies, etc.) can cause difficulty for children with ASD. They tend to use more nouns and labels but need help with action words, modifiers, and other relational words, as well as words with multiple meanings and figurative language.

- **Children with ASD have problems analyzing language in terms of situational contexts**, including the knowledge and beliefs of the speaker and the relationship between speaker and listener.

- **These children tend to use less-advanced gestures**, like pulling or leading, as opposed to showing, waving, and pointing.

- **The difficulty that children on the autistic spectrum have with symbolic play** (the ability to give and take during play) limits their ability to learn language and impacts their relationships with peers.

- **Children with ASD have scattered literacy skills.** They may have strong decoding and sight word abilities but can have poor comprehension and inferencing skills.

- **Children with ASD may have trouble telling relevant from irrelevant information.**

- **Finally, these children often exhibit poor executive functioning** (challenges in problem solving, self-organizing, time management, and completing multistep tasks, and the ability to plan, think, and reflect).

Behavioral and Emotional Regulation

Children with ASD have a hard time returning to "normal" behavior once they begin to lose control. They may use idiosyncratic strategies for self-regulation, such as rocking, vocal play, bolting, tantrums, and aggression. They have a hard time learning how to negotiate a break when they need one. They find it difficult to be flexible and to "go with the flow." The best solution to these issues is to build in opportunities for the child to appropriately express his needs until a successful behavior plan has been put in place.

Speech

As many as 30% to 50% of individuals with ASD do not develop functional verbal communication. They have trouble with articulation—the ability to say sounds in our language—resulting in a phonological delay. They may suffer from apraxia that ranges from limited speech to being nonverbal. They struggle with fluency in speech and writing. They have strange features in their speech, including poor pitch modulation and lack of intonation.

Unconventional Verbal Behavior

Additionally, children with ASD often have issues such as immediate echolalia (the immediate repetition of words) or delayed echolalia (imitation that is three turns or later in conversation), both of which may be communicative in nature. They may also have perseverative speech—words and sounds made in a cyclical, recurring manner. Children with ASD may also question their communication partners incessantly.

Strategies to Improve Communication

Improving communication with the child with ASD goes hand in hand with improving his academic capabilities and his peer relationships, as well as managing his behavior. Use these simple ideas to help him learn to communicate better. As you work on communication, be wary of making the child feel a need to demonstrate readiness skills. Also, keep the child's abilities in perspective and do not expect his skills to be the same as those of his classmates.

1. **Gain the student's attention before speaking.** A prearranged, perhaps nonverbal signal from you can help him learn when he needs to focus on you.

2. **Speak in clearly articulated sentences.** Use stress, intonation, and pauses to clarify or emphasize your meaning.

3. **Adjust the complexity of your language.** Use simpler sentence structures and topics.

4. **Allow the child sufficient processing time.**

5. **Model use of declarative language for the child to emulate.** Try using:
   - Comments (It is a beautiful, sunny day!)
   - Predictions (I think I know what will happen next in the story.)
   - Reflections (It was fun to sing together.)
   - Regulation (I am feeling hungry for lunch.)
   - Narrative (I am putting the boat in the water.)

6. **Avoid using more directive language such as questions, commands, and requests, in order to make fewer demands on the child.** For example, instead of saying, "Joey, put your jacket on," say, "It is time for everyone to put on a jacket." Then, give the child enough time to respond appropriately.

7. **Work in natural learning environments since context helps with generalizations.** For example, give a lesson on caring for books in the library as you are handling books with the class.

8. **Motivate the child by giving her meaningful choices that honor preferences.** For example, if you are sorting manipulatives, let her choose which kind to sort. This motivates her to do the activity and develops rapport.

9. **Give the child the ability to end or refuse some activities.**

10. **Always work toward generalizing skills across settings, with people, and in contexts.** From the example on page 46 (episodic memory), when you teach a new word like *roll,* create opportunities for the child to use it by giving her many things to roll besides the truck.

11. **Preteach new concepts and content vocabulary before teaching it in large groups.**

12. **Frequently model your expectations to provide additional visual supports.**

13. **Add picture schedules and give visual reminders of each lesson's essential questions and concepts.**

14. **For nonverbal children, the IEP team should consider implementing adaptive alternative communication**—This is a system of sign language, picture symbols, and written cues—to help develop a functional communication program.

15. **Teach the student how to ask for help by using written cue cards or picture cards.**

16. **Use snacktime and mealtimes, usually a situation when the child is very motivated, to develop vocabulary.** Teach words like *I, want, more, no, yes, yucky, yummy,* and *please.*

17. **Computerized instruction can also help with vocabulary, sentence structure, written responses, and social problem solving.**

18. **Create opportunities for peer interactions and play to inspire peer communication.**

19. **Select a different peer each week or month as a communication "role model" for the child with ASD.** Depending on the peer's maturity level, she can help narrate classroom instructions (for example, saying, "Here is the orange crayon," etc.), role-play social scenarios with the child, and model your instructions.

20. **Try team activities.** Many children will work harder for the success of a group than they would when working alone. Children with ASD can practice the interpersonal skills required to work effectively with different individuals as they achieve essential learning outcomes.

21. **The IEP team should work closely with the family by implementing a parent-training component.** This will enable parents to reinforce strategies to facilitate communication with their child. Be sure that parents' concerns, priorities, and perspectives are considered.

Fostering socialization and communication can be truly challenging, but few things are more rewarding than seeing a child with ASD learn to play or figure out how to ask appropriately for what he wants. An additional bonus is that mastery of communication skills, especially when combined with an appropriate classroom and curriculum and a sensory diet, can vastly improve the child's behavior.

However, as you move toward progress in all of these areas, there will always be "in between times" when the child is struggling to achieve a new IEP goal. Communication will break down, peer relationships will suffer, new classroom modifications will need to be implemented, and new sensory activities will need to be added to the IEP. During these times, and especially at the beginning of the school year, children with ASD may exhibit behavioral issues. Read Chapter Seven for more information about how to deal with disruptive behaviors that cannot always be managed ahead of time.

Chapter Seven
Beyond the Sensory Diet: Behavior Modification

Even though classroom and curriculum adjustments and the sensory diet are in place, the child with ASD may still have behavioral issues that diminish learning and appropriate socialization skill development. It is your job, and that of the IEP team, to discover what is causing the behavior and decide how best to manage and prevent it.

Consider Sources other than ASD

Children with ASD are all different, just like children who are not on the autism spectrum. Before attributing any behavior solely to the child's disability, remember that other things can cause poor behavior in all students, including this child. Illness, uncomfortable clothing, an adverse reaction to a food eaten, lack of sleep, separation anxiety, abrupt changes in weather, and poor peer relationships can all upset the child with ASD as they can any other child.

Your attitude can also affect the child's behavior. If you are wondering why the child seems agitated and upset, remember that he may be wondering the same thing about you. Your stress or illness can easily overflow in the classroom. If you thrive on change and have a teaching style that is not predictable and consistent, that can disrupt the child. And, personality clashes may occur, especially with a child with ASD since she may not have the skills to be a model student and will need your special effort to succeed in the classroom. Even if you do not like the child, or are bothered by her behavior, it is absolutely inappropriate not to act professionally and perform the job that you were hired to do. If you simply cannot bring yourself to deal fairly and even lovingly with this child, you must either find a way to rise above these feelings, or you need to talk to your administrators about possibly making a change.

When NOT to Attempt to Modify Behavior

If after considering (and remedying) the above possible causes of poor behavior, unacceptable behaviors still exist, you should begin observing the child and recording data from each behavior episode. The first question you should ask yourself is: Does the behavior occur incessantly? If so, it can be attributed to a sensory motor processing problem and is part of the child's overall profile. In this case, the IEP team should reinvestigate the child's sensory needs and try to manage the behavior by finding a substitute. The team must realize that if the child requires the behavior in order to function, it will be very difficult to eliminate.

Due to the nature of ASD, behavioral difficulties should be handled individually and not based on a global philosophy of punishment or discipline. When the child's brain becomes disorganized, do not immediately respond with punishment. Disciplining a "sensory seeker" by taking away privileges, recess, or other opportunities to move will intensify those random movements, fidgeting, and outbursts. Punishment may also be a bad idea for those children with ASD who are high-functioning enough to realize they are "different." These children may have a strong desire to fit in with their peers. Punishment will only lower their self-esteem even further. Instead of punishment, the child with ASD needs something (a break, the sensory diet, or some other assistance) that will help him regain his composure. Not only will he learn to seek help to moderate his own behavior, his self-esteem will improve because of his accomplishment in doing so.

Documenting Behaviors

Keep a behavior diary at your desk in which to record and review your data and observations. If the behavior is not incessant, you then need to ask:

- Does the behavior seem to cluster around a certain time or times of the day?

- Might the behavior be communicating hunger, thirst, a need for a break, difficulty with transitions, or high (unrealistic) demands?

- Does the behavior occur primarily when a particular person is present? If so, does the student desire attention or escape from that person?

- Does the behavior occur when a specific stimulus is present (for example, when the PA system comes on)?

- Does the behavior occur during specific activities? If so, are those activities too easy, too hard, highly desirable, or least favorite?

- Where does the behavior occur? Are there specific places where it is more likely to occur than others?

- When and where does the behavior not occur? For example, if it occurs every day at 11:00 except on Tuesdays, and you realize that on Tuesdays the child is allowed to purchase his lunch, then you have a clue about what may be causing the behavior.

After you have collected your data, take it to the IEP team. Discuss what is happening, outline what changes you would like to see, and present any suggestions you have for making those changes happen. You and the team should list any change on the IEP.

Changing the Behavior

A common error is to assume that behavior problems can be corrected without doing something to change the brain dysfunction producing these behaviors. It is easy to recognize unpleasant behavior, but it is much more difficult to recognize the dysfunction in the nervous system organization that underlies that behavior. Assessing and collecting information on behaviors that impede progress and participation in the LRE is a priority.

Once the behavior(s) are well documented, the IEP team can create a behavior plan from the information you have collected. The plan will be in addition to other modifications you have already made, including the sensory diet. It should have structure and continuity and be designed to meet the unique needs of the child, and all professionals working with the child should know how to follow the plan. The plan should also not become part of the problem. Behavior plans often have demands and requirements for expected behaviors, which can actually impede the facilitation of appropriate behavior. With the team, ensure that the expected behaviors of the plan are within the developmental capabilities of the child.

Also enlist parents' help by asking them to suggest reinforcers that are highly motivating for the child. Parents will have a lot of information to share on this subject, and school teams can insert the most desired reinforcers and plan for when to use them.

Once the plan is in place, be consistent when dealing with unwanted behaviors within the classroom. Carefully follow the protocol within the behavior plan and ask parents to do the same as much as possible.

The following are general strategies to remember when planning the behavior modification plan. Again, use these in addition to the strategies on the IEP that are already in place.

1. **Use role-playing as a strategy to develop appropriate behavior.**

2. **Classroom rules can be a source of stress for the child with ASD. The more rules you have, the more likely that the child will "break" them.** The best use of rules is when they are guidelines, not barriers to success. Develop rules with students, make as few as possible, and keep them short and clear for easy understanding.

3. **Provide clear, concise expectations and consequences for rule breaking that match the child's ability to understand in order to achieve the desired behavior.** Make sure the consequences are clearly understood and consistently enforced. They should be immediate, consistent, and specific. For example, if a child misbehaves in PE, do not wait until after the class to enact a consequence. Children with ASD need to know the exact behavior that is being targeted.

4. **Make a positive, personal comment every time the child with ASD shows any evidence of interest. Use praise generously.** Speak privately, without the audience of peers, when you have to point out the child's inappropriate behavior.

5. **Provide the student with alternatives. Intersperse short work periods with breaks, physical activities, or change of tasks, and let her choose between two or more options.** She will feel that she has more control over the environment and may be less likely to act out.

6. **Similarly, go further to modify the child's schedule and offer her a chance to select activities throughout the day.** This will give her a chance to make her own schedule. Such as letting her select her own desk, this gives the child the opportunity to let you know what is comfortable to her.

7. **Consider how much time you spend reinforcing and practicing skills.** With other children you can keep explaining until they "get it." Repetition can have the opposite effect on a child with ASD and make her agitated. Consider using different avenues to reinforce a skill. For example, let her recite a poem or act out a story, instead of writing it down.

8. **Revisit the curriculum with the IEP team.** Even after the IEP team makes adjustments, if the child perceives curriculum demands to be too hard, she may behave unenthusiastically and avoid tasks, especially when the IEP team has designed strategies to keep her on task. To reduce the child's frustration, follow the strategies listed in Chapter Four: The Learning Environment (page 15), including providing an overview before starting a task, breaking

assignments into shorter segments, increasing time allotted to complete assignments, using concrete examples of concepts before teaching the abstract, providing a finished example or a template of a completed assignment, monitoring the student's comprehension of directions, slowing the rate of instruction, varying academic material to keep it interesting, and providing visual and kinesthetic modes of instruction in addition to auditory.

9. **Interrupting the flow of events can help stop unacceptable behaviors without having a confrontation. Use these strategies to interrupt behavior:**
   - Give the child extra attention in case she is acting out of a need for it.

   - Remind the child of the consequences of her actions.

   - Clarify reality for the child by explaining the possible outcomes of her actions (beyond any disciplinary measures). For example, if a child is getting ready to throw a pencil at a classmate, explain that the pencil will hurt the classmate, and she will be sad.

   - Communicate expected behavior—make sure the child knows what she is supposed to do.

   - Provide reassurance. If she is unsure of what to do, prompt her and praise her for following through.

   - Model appropriate behavior and point out the behavior of classmates who are behaving well. The child with ASD may not be able to register others' emotions, but she may be able to catalog images of appropriate behaviors in her mind and emulate them when similar situations arise.

10. **Use ignoring, redirecting, reinforcing, and rewarding as intervention techniques. Ignoring techniques:**
    - Plan to ignore certain behaviors that are not dangerous and that will not escalate to dangerous levels. This includes low-level behaviors that the child needs to process sensory information. Continue to acknowledge the child, but act as if the behavior is not taking place.

    - Devalue negative behavior by displaying no reaction. This discourages the child from using the behavior to get a reaction.

    - Keep calm and show little emotion. Remember, you need not react immediately unless someone is in danger of being hurt, so take a moment to think out your response.

11. **Redirecting as an intervention technique:**
    - If the child is reasonably under control, use verbal persuasion and ask her to cease the behavior.

    - Provide opportunities for the child to vent by taking him outside the classroom as needed.

    - Ahead of time, offer help with difficult tasks so that the child knows you will not let him struggle.

- Introduce new behaviors that are incompatible to the undesirable ones. For example, if the student likes to grab people when walking down the hallway, ask her to carry something that requires two hands.

- Increase physical activities in order to dissipate the child's destructive energy.

12. **Rewarding and reinforcing as an intervention technique:**
   - Offer praise; look for ways to reward the child for appropriate behaviors.

   - Be affectionate. Children will try harder for people who like them.

   - Use non-verbal attention and prearrange special programs and incentives acknowledging appropriate behavior. For example, place a box of treats in the classroom. If the child is able to behave all day, she should know to help herself to a treat from the box. Only direct her verbally if she loses that privilege.

Intervention Programs

There are a number of professional intervention programs that can be utilized in an educational setting, including Applied Behavior Analysis (ABA), The Floortime Foundation, Relationship Development Intervention, TEACCH, and Verbal Behavioral Intervention. All have some similar features, but all have differences, as well. The IEP team should review the scope and depth of each program and determine which best meets the unique needs of the child.

In some cases, more than one type of intervention should be used, as any one program may have aspects that do not meet all of the needs of the children. The IEP team must see the child as a unique individual. Limiting intervention to one program without determining whether it is a complete match can actually impede the development of appropriate behavior. When a program has been selected, it must be constantly under review and scrutiny. If it is not, compliance to the program then becomes the focus, rather than the child.

With these programs, carry over to home is critical for providing the continuity and structure that the child needs to attain the goals desired. Parents must be willing to enforce the behavior plan. The OT, PT, and paraprofessionals should also be trained in the selected program so that they can be valuable participants in her ongoing development.

What to Do about Some Specific Behaviors

Children with ASD are different, and so each child's behaviors are also certain to be different. However, the behaviors listed below are among the most likely to be present and can be disruptive or hinder the child from socializing and learning.

The child with ASD may continue to **perseverate** (flap his hands, handle objects repeatedly, rock, hum, etc.) for long periods of time. For example, the child may be focused on bouncing a ball for an hour. You or a paraprofessional can intervene by trying to roll the ball back and forth, catching the ball if appropriate, or removing the ball from the child and trying to introduce a new activity.

The child may also continue to **fixate**—demonstrate an interest in something external. If the child is beginning to self-stimulate on this idea or thought, changing the activity or introducing some other project that the child usually enjoys can be successful in helping move beyond his fixation temporarily. A more successful approach is to use the motivation and interests of the child to lead him to *want* to relate to the external world. To refer to the previous example of a favorite cartoon character, use the character as a segue way to other activities. Make up math problems that involve the character, have the child write about the character, or offer a board game with the character's picture in order to help him move into another realm of activities.

You may observe a child demonstrating task avoidance (or avoiding a person or environment) by running away. **Flight behaviors** may be caused by the child's desire to escape from tasks that carry a sensory component he perceives as challenging or threatening. In those cases you may be able to determine through observation which sensory input is causing the issue. Ask the professionals on the IEP team to help you brainstorm ways to desensitize the child to the sensory component he finds threatening. For example, a child who runs away from the lunch line may be afraid of the hallway that leads to the lunchroom. You can help the child walk past the hallway. Then, use something the child finds motivating, such as a favorite toy or special snack, to entice him to walk further and further down the hall until he reaches the lunchroom.

Another behavior sometimes observed in children with ASD is what teachers and parents perceive as **calculating or manipulative behavior**. This can occur when a child has exceptional language and conversation skills but is "typically" autistic in other areas. For example, the child with ASD may resort to verbally challenging teachers and parents and asking, "Why?" Adults often feel that a child who communicates well is not actually experiencing fear of sensory experiences, and so they conclude that the behaviors (tantrums, etc.) must be manipulative rather than genuine. The reality is that such behaviors are more likely efforts to avoid, control, and manipulate situations, tasks, or places he finds threatening. It is important to remember to use the child's ability to communicate to his advantage and yours. After a tantrum, talk with the child about what caused his tantrum. It is imperative to assist the child in understanding how and why sensory input is impacting him, and, in turn, this may diminish the controlling and scheming behaviors. It may take several conversations to understand what the child is reacting to, but once you do, you can take action. Make a list of words and phrases the child can use to tell you how he is feeling. Make your own list of times when the behavior is likely to occur, as a reminder. Then, work together with the IEP team and the child to deal with these situations more appropriately.

Finally, some behaviors, especially flight behaviors, may escalate into **aggression** (biting, hitting, or scratching) if the child feels he cannot get away. Preventing and redirecting the behavior is still important, but more action is needed in order to protect other children and staff. The first order of business is putting a plan in place with the IEP team. All staff members who work with the child should know the protocol for managing that physical behavior. If necessary, in-service training and professional development workshops about autism and physical aggression should be available to the staff. If physical aggression becomes unmanageable and unsafe to others, it is critical that the staff members can protect themselves and others in the room. If the child cannot be removed from the room, then the others in the room should be removed at that time for everyone's safety.

Conclusion

With all there is to consider when including a child with ASD in a regular education classroom, you, the child, the parents, and other staff are going to feel overwhelmed at times. It helps to keep in mind your primary responsibilities: to provide a safe and nurturing classroom in which the child can access the curriculum and work to his best abilities; to accept and understand the impact of this disability; and to make sure that the child's learning environment meets his present needs. It is not your responsibility to make the child with ASD someone he is not. Rather, simply welcome and support him in all his endeavors and treat him with respect and dignity at his present level of performance. This is no more or less than you would do for any other child.

Appendix A:
The IEP Meeting–Hints for Parents of Children Who May Be on the Autism Spectrum

As you read this, you may be at several different points on the timeline of your child's development. You or a teacher may suspect your child has an autism spectrum disorder, and assessments are just beginning. You may have a confirmed diagnosis. You may be preparing for your first (or your tenth) IEP meeting. Or, your autistic child's new teacher has passed this information to you. Wherever you are on the journey, you are now an advocate—a conduit between the school and the child—and a team member who must rely on other IEP team members to help you do what is best for your child. Here are some ideas to make these meetings go smoothly:

- Recognize and accept the diagnosis and issues your child presents. This is far easier said than done, but it moves you in the direction of knowing what your child needs and makes you a powerful IEP team member.

- Be aware of your communication skills. Are you threatening, intimidating, unapproachable, or do you present yourself as likeable, informative, and amiable? Consider the effect on others of how you communicate.

- Develop harmonious relationships with the teachers and staff who work closely with your child so that your child is the focus, not the personalities involved.

- Develop a system for how the school will communicate with you.

- Help the IEP team develop a sensory diet and a behavior plan if either is needed, and ask an IEP team member to visit your home and help you implement the plan. A visit from an occupational therapist or other professional can determine other home changes that can help.

- Since we cannot "see" sensory integrative dysfunction, it is easy to forget that the child has a disability. Have realistic expectations for your child's sake. Point out your child's strengths and use them to build his self-esteem.

- Explore activities that your child can engage in successfully, and keep your expectations realistic so that all family members can enjoy themselves.

- To convey a point or to convince people to try new things, give factual information about your child's needs, explain why you want something done, and then suggest how to do it. Focus on finding solutions rather than naming causes.

- Be reasonable. Try to keep things in perspective, and your emotions in check. It is easy to become defensive and not "allow" yourself to hear information presented. If you get overwhelmed, ask for a break, and then rejoin the discussion.

- Changes, modifications, additions, and deletions to your child's IEP can be made at any time during the school year if things are not moving in the right direction.

- Knowledge is power, so do your homework. Provide materials that can focus the team on your child's needs. Understand the law and your rights (you may bring an educated advocate to assist you) as recommendations are being presented.

- Share outside evaluations of your child. If an outside evaluation's findings conflict with those that the school has performed, listen to all facts before making a plan. (Often the mindset is that when you pay for an outside evaluation it holds more weight than the school's evaluation. Rather than using evaluation findings to try to discredit the school, draw from both to make the best plan for your child.)

- Educate your child from the bottom to the top; trust those who have daily hands-on experiences with your child. Direct your questions to them, even if other "high-ranking" professionals have joined the meeting. This ensures that your child's needs, not school policy or district philosophy, govern the planning of the appropriate educational program.

- Remember that if the IEP strategy includes therapy, it needs to be given sufficient time to work since children all develop at their own rates.

- Remember that teachers and staff work very hard on behalf of your child. Even if you don't agree with the methods that are being used, if your child is improving, recognize it by writing or calling to say thank you when things are going well.

- If you feel that decisions are being made without you, call and ask to be included in discussions. You can suggest a "pre" IEP meeting to talk about your ideas and goals for your child so that members can think about solutions ahead of time.

- Investigate networking with other families and joining support groups through the school and outside of it. Sharing information can be helpful and comforting.

- When you are consumed and overwhelmed by the present, look towards the future. It may be unrealistic and unfair to assume that you can "fix" all of your child's issues. Micromanaging some issues can cause only weaknesses to be addressed while removing opportunities to build on strengths.

- Seek professional assistance through school personnel or otherwise if you need more information, assessments, or family counseling for coping strategies.

Advocates

If you feel overwhelmed with your child's diagnosis or feel that you may not be able to get her needs addressed, consider employing an advocate to assist you during the IEP process. An advocate will help you understand information shared at the IEP meeting and can make sure your concerns are heard and addressed. A good advocate:

- Has credentials and knowledge concerning the education of the child with ASD.

- Has researched ASD and how the diagnosis applies to your child.

- Has observed your child in the educational setting and at home.

- Has interviewed teachers and other professionals about the strengths and weaknesses of the child's daily program

- Comes to the IEP meetings with an open mind, not an agenda to push through

- Seeks an amicable and harmonious atmosphere in the meeting.

What to Bring to an IEP Meeting

Sharing information year after year with new IEP teams can be exhausting. Facilitate this process by creating a portfolio about your child and family. Each year, update it by adding and deleting information. Present the portfolio to IEP team members well in advance of each meeting. The portfolio can include the following:

- A current photo of your child and family members

- A brief family history and notes about how your child interacts with your family.

- A page naming the actual diagnosis. Include a list of the syndrome's basic characteristics that apply to your child.

- A list of your child's strengths and weaknesses, likes and dislikes, what motivates your child, and any other helpful information, including your thoughts and concerns.

- A copy of the present IEP, and also the past two IEPs, if possible.

- Evaluations and reports from all staff members who have worked with your child, as well as outside evaluations.

- Medical reports that list medical impacts on your child's educational performance.

- A list of medications, dosing routines, side effects, and any other information about how medicines affect your child.

- A statement of your present and future desires for your child. If your child can articulate them, include a list from her, as well.

Appendix B:
Autism and Play—A Guide for Parents

Since most children play adequately without parental assistance and since play's role in brain development is not straightforward, most people think of play as mere entertainment. However, play is just as important for a child's overall development as schoolwork. Concepts necessary for most daily functions as well as formal learning are best developed through play.

If a child does not play with as many different things as other children, parents may think that he just is not interested in that type of play. However, the child who is not interested in normal play may have a sensory processing disorder. For a child with autism, interactions with people and objects (such as toys) can be very difficult. For the child with dyspraxia, play is very limited because he has trouble with motor planning. When a child does not respond to directions (up, down, under, over, etc.) he may not possess knowledge of those concepts. The child with a vestibular (inner ear) system dysfunction is restricted by input that he cannot modulate. The tactile defensive child may avoid playing with other children because he does not want them to invade his personal space. In a safe and nurturing environment, parents and teachers of children with autism spectrum disorders (ASD) can respond to these issues through play.

The essential goal to be attained through play is the child's expression of his inner drive toward self-fulfillment as a sensory-motor being. When the child follows his inner drive to produce physical activity, he masters his environment and his body part function. Physical activity produces sensory stimulation and adaptive responses that assist in organizing the brain.

The parts of our brains that direct the desire to initiate movement, respond to sensory stimuli, or do something new or different and that tell the muscles how to move the body, generally function well. This system may not work efficiently for the child with ASD, which can cause his play to consist only of simple actions repeated for long periods of time. More complex or new actions do not occur to him or are resisted by him.

Other parts of the brain register the potential use of many things. For example, riding a tricycle requires a fair amount of abstract thinking as the child determines how to sit on the trike, where to place his feet, and how to make the pedals go around, as well as the understanding that moving the pedals will move the tricycle. The child with ASD may not be able to do this type of thinking; even if he sees a tricycle, he still may not realize that it is something to ride. He may resist if anyone tries to get him to sit on the tricycle.

Through play, all children receive sensory input from their bodies, and from gravity, that is essential for motor and emotional development. The sensory input makes it fun. All locomotor and nonlocomotor play produces vestibular, proprioceptive, and tactile input. Children play to receive this input. The more the child plays, the more his senses are stimulated, and the more he must produce complex adaptive responses.

As a child with ASD plays, he moves his body parts in countless ways, and the sensations from these movements create new sensory maps of his body and he stores them in his brain. Through gross motor movements, he learns how to relate himself to the space around him. Through manipulation of small play items, he learns to use his hands and fingers efficiently. The benefits of these play skills pave the way for increased opportunities in communication and social development, and for increased competence.

Here is a list of ideas for increased physical activity. Through trial and error, you will learn that the activities your child enjoys are the activities that he needs in order to increase physical competence, so let your child lead the way through his responses. However, never stop encouraging your child to try new things.

- Make physical activity a regular part of family life rather than trying to "fit it in." Include activities that the child with ASD and all other family members enjoy.

- Activities do not have to be competitive. Modify them so that each family member enjoys success.

- Comfortable clothing can enhance the activity, especially for the child with ASD.

- Always stretch before vigorous activities. It warms up the muscles and helps mentally prepare the child with ASD for transitioning to a physical activity.

- Designate appropriate indoor and outdoor areas of the home as play areas so that your child with ASD knows where to go to indicate that he wants to play.

- For holidays and birthdays, encourage relatives and friends to purchase simple toys and equipment that promote physical activity. The fact that they are gifts will make your child excited to use them.

- For birthday parties, build in a physical theme such as miniature golf, bowling, or swimming.

- Include extended family members and friends when engaging in physical activities to encourage variety.

- Ask your child's teacher how much physical activity/recess/social time is included in the school day. Advocate for these periods in your child's IEP.

- Volunteer to assist the classroom teacher in providing greater opportunities for physical activity during the day.

- Use community resources such as local recreation centers, playgrounds, parks, hiking and bike trails, and swimming pools for children's play opportunities. Seek out those that provide special programs for children with disabilities.

- Hook up with friends so that if you are too busy for play, your child may still have the opportunity to fulfill the need for movement.

- Park far away from the entrances of stores, the library, and other destinations to encourage more walking and talking.

- Incorporate appropriate chores for the child with ASD into his family life.

- When appropriate, volunteer yourself and your child to assist an elderly neighbor with simple yard cleanup.

- Make sure the child with ASD is dressed appropriately and play in the snow.

- Plant a flower or vegetable garden. Have each family member do a different task, like weeding, digging, and watering.

- Take long family walks and take the dog if you have one. If the dog is calm enough, let the child with ASD hold the leash for deep pressure input.

- Try kite flying. The pull of the kite string is a great deep pressure activity.

- Camping promotes all types of physical activity: walking, hiking, gathering wood, swimming, and paddling.

- Visit a local farm to pick your own fruits and vegetables.

- Plan a treasure hunt in the yard.

- Provide a variety of balls for your child to explore and play with.

- Croquet, tag, hide-and-seek, and boccie are easy activities to modify and make appropriate for the child with ASD.

- Hopscotch, shooting baskets, and jumping rope are old standbys that help children acquire gravitational security and balance.

- Wash the car together as a family instead of taking it to a car wash.

- Explore martial arts to help your child improve coordination and balance, as well as posture and gait.

- Let your child dance to different types of music.

- Encourage your child to act out a story or play charades, if he is capable.

References

American Speech-Language-Hearing Association. 2006. Guidelines for speech-language pathologists in diagnosis, assessment and treatment of autism spectrum disorders across the life span. http://www.asha.org/docs/html/GL2006-00049.html.

American Speech-Language-Hearing Association. 2006. Principles for speech-language pathologists in diagnosis, assessment, and treatment of autism spectrum disorders across the life span. http://www.asha.org/docs/html/TR2006-00143.html.

American Speech-Language-Hearing Association. 2006. Roles and responsibilities of speech-language pathologists in diagnosis, assessment, and treatment of autism spectrum disorders across the life span. http://www.asha.org/docs/html/PS2006-00105.html.

Ayres, A. J. 1979. *Sensory integration and the child*. Los Angeles: Western Psychology Service.

Benbow, M. 1990. *Loops and other groups, a kinesthetic writing system*. Tuscon, AZ: Therapy Skill Builders.

Erhardt, R. P. 1992. Eye-hand coordination. In *Development of hand skills in the child*, ed. J. Case-Smith and C. Pehoski, 13–22. Bethesda, MD: The American Occupational Therapy Association.

Exner, C. E. 1992. In-hand manipulation skills. In *Development of hand skills in the child*, ed. J. Case-Smith and C. Pehoski, 35–45. Bethesda, MD: The American Occupational Therapy Association.

National Association for Sport and Physical Education. 99 tips for family fitness fun. http://www.shapeup.org/pubs/99tips/started.html.

National Education Association. 2006. The puzzle of autism. http://www.nea.org/specialed/nearesources-specialed.html.

Lord, C., and McGee, J. P., eds. 2001. Educating children with autism. Washington, DC: National Academy Press.

Sensorimotor foundations of academic ability. 1975. In *Perceptual and learning disabilities in children,* vol. 2, ed. W. M. Cruickshank and D. P. Hallahan, 300-360. New York: Syracuse University Press.

Trott, Maryann Colby. 2002. Oh behave!: Sensory processing and behavioral strategies. Therapy Skill Builders.

U.S. Department of Education. 1997, 2004. *Individuals with disabilities education act, Amendments of 1997*. http://idea.ed.gov/.

Weikart, Phyllis S., and Carlton, Elizabeth B. 1995. Foundations in elementary education: Movement. Ypsilanti, MI: High/Scope Press.